A Fiction Lover's Devotional

21 Days
of Joy

Stories
that
Celebrate
Mom

BroadStreet
PUBLISHING

Published by BroadStreet Publishing Group, LLC
Racine, Wisconsin, USA
www.broadstreetpublishing.com

21 Days of Joy
Stories that Celebrate Mom

ISBN: 978-1-4245-5227-6 (hardcover)
ISBN: 978-1-4245-5228-3 (e-book)

Cover design by Chris Garborg at www.garborgdesign.com.
Interior by Katherine Lloyd at www.TheDESKonline.com.

Stock or custom editions of BroadStreet Publishing titles may be purchased in bulk for educational, business, ministry, fundraising, or sales promotional use. For information, please e-mail info@broadstreetpublishing.com.

Printed in China

Contents

by Deborah Raney

The subject of Mother's Day brings a mingling of emotions. Not all of us are mothers, but all of us have or at least had a mother. Whether we knew her or not, whether our relationship was warm and fuzzy or cool and distant, each of us was brought into this world by a woman who wore the label "Mother."

If you were raised by a wonderful mom, you are blessed. If your mom is still living and active in your life, you are blessed beyond words.

The Ten Commandments exhort us to honor our mothers and to not forget their teachings. For me, that's easy. I was blessed with a loving, caring, godly mother who taught my brother and three sisters and me to cherish one another, to honor her and Daddy, and to obey God's Word. Today we all live in the same town, and while my mother's health and mind are failing rapidly, she continues to be a source of joy and comfort to me.

One of my mother's greatest gifts was introducing me to the joy of story. I had severe asthma as a child, which meant

I was often left out of the outdoor activities on the farm. It could have been a lonely childhood, but my mother turned it into a blessing by taking me to the library each week and reading every book we came home with. Not only did I learn about the world, but I learned of God's love as well.

I am also blessed to *be* a mother. Although doctors told me as a young teenager that I probably would not be able to conceive, God had a different plan. My two sons and two daughters are the greatest blessings in my life.

Even if you've lost your mother to death, or some circumstance prevents you from having a relationship with the woman who gave birth to you or adopted you, there are likely other women in your life who have fulfilled some of the roles of a mother. And even if you don't have children, you may very well be a mother figure in someone's life.

God's diversity in assigning the role of "mother" is as varied and creative as He is. Our neighbor up the road from the farm where I grew up had no children of her own, but she "adopted" every neighborhood child, making each of us feel welcome in her home and throwing a cookie-baking party for us every Christmas. If I hadn't had a mother, Jewel would have filled that role beautifully. There are many other children, now grown, who will never forget the kindness and motherly affection Jewel poured out over the years.

The book of Isaiah speaks of God's love being like that of a mother who comforts her child. That certainly places a mother's love in high esteem.

Whether you've been the recipient of such love, the giver

of such love, or both, you are blessed. And if you've not experienced one or the other from an earthly perspective, take comfort in knowing that God loves you and wants to gather you to Himself as a mother hen gathers her brood (Luke 13:34). Cherish the motherly love you give and receive, but more importantly, be secure in the love of the God who created you and gave you life, for that is the greatest story any of us will ever have to tell.

1

If Only

by Anne Mateer

Jessica slid another cookie from the package and brought it to her mouth, almost without thought. Two days until the law firm's twenty-fifth anniversary party and still she had nothing to wear. Another cookie found its way to Jessica's lips. She *did* have half a dozen dresses hanging in her closet, but none of them would do. The other women would wear dazzling outfits with designer labels, their feet encased in strappy sandals with price tags higher than Jessica's monthly grocery budget.

Another cookie crunched between her teeth. She looked down at the plastic tray and scowled. Thin, flower-shaped butter cookies. The kind that cost a dollar a package. She'd thought that by the time John reached his fourth year as an associate in the law firm she'd have moved beyond cheap pre-school snacks.

After sealing the remaining cookies in a plastic bag,

Jessica put them in the pantry. One day she'd be able to buy the good stuff. Pepperidge Farm Milanos. Even Oreos would satisfy. Something other than the most inexpensive item in the snack aisle.

A whimper from the back of the house let her know Josh was awake. She smiled, in spite of her grumpiness. How could she lament a nice dress and shoes when she had a baby instead? Finally. After five years of trying. Four failed in vitro procedures. Three years waiting to adopt. Putting every spare penny—and some not-so-spare pennies—toward their dream of a family.

Jessica lifted Josh from his crib and cradled him. "Hush now, little man. Mama's here."

Mama. Her heart swelled every time she realized God had granted the dream of her heart.

She kissed Josh's warm cheek, carried him to his high chair in the kitchen, and pulled out his favorite snack. He banged his hands on the tray, eager for the small cubes of cheese she scattered within his reach. He popped one in his mouth.

Jessica sighed. If only she could have Josh *and* a nice outfit. Like the other women she'd see at the firm party. They all had children—many had more than one—but they never seemed to lack anything for themselves. Maybe if she went back to work, made some money just for her.

"Ma-ma-ma." Josh slapped at the empty tray, grinning.

But going back to work would mean leaving her baby, missing the days she wanted so much to enjoy. She picked up a cereal box and shook a few oat rings into the palm of her hand. Not Cheerios. Too expensive. The knock-off brand. Just like her wardrobe.

"Annalee, come back here this instant!" Belinda hated the screech in her voice but saw no alternative. She refused to let her daughter out of the house looking like—well, a streetwalker.

The teenager didn't even turn her head. She slung her backpack over one shoulder and slammed the door behind her. The hum of the garage door preceded the roar of Annalee's Mustang, which Rick had given her on her sixteenth birthday. Tires screeched as she peeled out of the driveway and onto the street. Then the noise faded to silence.

Belinda clenched her hands into fists. This wasn't the life she'd signed up for twenty-four years ago when she said "I do" on a warm May evening, the moon glowing over ocean waves lapping the beach. Love, honor, and cherish. Ha! Rick hadn't done those things since he gave himself body and soul to a six-figure salary at a prestigious law firm. He spent weekends working—or fishing on his ridiculously expensive bass boat—instead of at home with Belinda. Or Annalee.

She sank onto the leather sofa and looked around. No dishes cluttered the granite countertops or the wide farm-house sink. No shoes littered the hand-scraped hardwood floors. Not even the throw pillows sat askew. Nothing out of order. Nothing out of place.

Nothing except every relationship in her life.

Belinda let herself sulk for five minutes. Then ten. A half

hour later, her phone buzzed. She rose, legs stiff, praying Annalee had texted. An apology would be amazing. A notice of her daughter's clothing receiving censure at school would do. But when she picked up her phone from the counter, the screen showed only a reminder.

Firm Anniversary Party. 7 p.m.

Belinda closed the screen, then poured herself another cup of coffee. She had a walk-in closet full of nice clothing, but today she needed a distraction. Something special to buoy her spirits. To allow her to play the part of gracious wife of the managing partner. She carried her coffee to her spacious bedroom, ready to plan her evening.

"Are you sure I look all right?" Jessica bit her bottom lip and turned to the full-length mirror attached to the back of the bedroom door.

From behind her, John slid his arms around her waist and kissed the base of her neck before meeting her gaze in the mirror. "You look fabulous." From his reflection, Jessica could tell he meant the compliment.

Warmth spread through her as she turned into his embrace. "Thank you." She pressed a kiss to his lips, then hugged him tight.

Of course, John didn't know the difference between an off-brand dress and one with a designer label. She doubted he'd notice that her outfit didn't measure up to the other women's tonight. But she would. And she wanted the approval of the other women. She ached to fit in. To feel part of their world. Or at least pretend to for an evening.

Jessica picked up the small black purse edged with rhinestones and followed John to the living room, where Deena, their babysitter, played patty-cake with Josh.

"We won't be too late," Jessica said.

John curled his hand over hers. "Unless we're having such a good time we can't pull ourselves away."

Deena laughed. "No problem. Josh and I will be fine."

Jessica knew it was true. And she was grateful. But as John held the car door open and she slid into his ten-year-old Camry, she couldn't help wishing her life had turned out a little bit different.

At the country club, Belinda stood next to Rick, greeting each attorney and spouse as they arrived at the party. A shimmery black dress hugged her curves and accentuated her long legs. Hours at the gym had paid off. And her stylist had worked a lovely up-do with her frosty-blonde hair. But her feet already ached in the four-inch Jimmy Choos. She'd slip them off for a little while once they sat down to dinner. Maybe give them to Annalee after the party.

"John, Jessica, how nice to see you." Belinda glanced over Jessica's outfit and frowned. Someone needed to teach that girl to shop. Another few years and John would be a partner. His wife couldn't go around looking as if the firm didn't give him adequate compensation.

Belinda leaned in for a quick hug and remembered that the couple had recently adopted a child. "And how is that little guy of yours?"

Jessica hesitated as her gaze roved over Belinda, cut to the floor, then lifted. "He's good." Her smile brightened. "Great, actually. We're so thankful to have him."

"I'm sure you are. A long-awaited gift." Belinda wished she still thought of Annalee as a gift.

"Yes, he is." John beamed.

When his gaze met his wife's, Belinda's heart constricted. What would it be like to start again? To have a little one. To do things differently. Especially if you could have a man who looked at you the way John looked at Jessica. He didn't seem to mind the obviously covered dark circles that ringed her eyes or the poorly cut dress that bulged in all the wrong places.

John's hand found the small of his wife's back. He led her toward the buffet table. Belinda glanced at Rick, who'd angled away from her, lost in conversation about a recent case. She'd give up the house, the clothes, the cars, and the vacations to have a relationship with her husband and her child.

Life Application

Exodus 20:17 tells us not to covet anything our neighbor has—house, spouse, children, transportation, or possessions. But in today's culture, we often desire the things, circumstances, or relationships we see in the lives of others. We think if we could just have what they have, we would finally be happy.

The truth is, a lack of things or relationships isn't what makes us dissatisfied. The problem lies within our hearts. When we covet, we are essentially saying, *God, I don't really trust You to provide the things I need. And I don't believe that You alone can give me peace and contentment.*

Matthew 6:33 says, "Seek first his kingdom and his righteousness, and all these things will be given to you as well."

How do we eliminate covetousness? By trusting God to provide. And then trusting that *what* He provides is everything we need to live a life pleasing to Him in whatever circumstances we find ourselves.

About the Author

Anne Mateer is the author of four historical novels and a contemporary short story in Guideposts' *A Cup of Christmas Cheer*, volume 4. Anne and her husband live in Texas and are the proud parents of three young adults. To find out more about Anne, visit her at annemateer.com.

2

Worthy of Praise

by Sherry Kyle

J stared into the eyes of my twelve-year-old daughter, wishing I could take her pain away. *Really, Lord? Braces and glasses at the same time?* How much can one middle-school girl take?

Even though Hannah had picked out designer frames, her expression told me she hated them, and no amount of compliments from me would change her mind.

We scheduled a follow-up appointment and walked to the car.

The spring promised new leaves on the trees, warmer air, and longer days, all things my daughter looked forward to and enjoyed, but today Hannah shuffled, her steps slow and measured.

"Wow, what a beautiful day!" I clicked the unlock button on the remote and slid inside our SUV. Hannah slunk into the passenger seat beside me. At least she didn't sit in the back.

Once on the road, I turned on the radio to my daughter's favorite Christian station and sang along, my shoulders moving in time to the beat.

Instead of joining in, Hannah stared out the window, still and quiet.

Lord, this is going to be harder than I thought.

I flipped off the radio and opened my window, welcoming the breeze.

"So, how was school today?" I immediately cringed. Stupid question. According to Hannah, every day was sheer torture. Too much drama. I racked my brain to think of a different topic of conversation.

I couldn't come up with a single thing. So I kept silent and prayed my daughter would make it all the way home before she burst into tears so I could gather her in my arms.

Kids need their space—and time to understand their feelings before they're able to verbalize them to anyone else. My girl might not even know how she felt about the new lenses sitting on the bridge of her nose. Frankly, I didn't know how I felt either. A little guilty, perhaps, since she inherited my less-than-perfect eyesight.

I pulled into the driveway, turned off the engine, and got out of the car, finally finding my voice. "Are you hungry? We could make smoothies. I just bought fresh strawberries, and we have orange juice and yogurt." I infused my tone with cheeriness, hoping my attitude would change Hannah's mood.

"No, thanks." She hooked her backpack over one shoulder. "I have a lot of homework. I'll be in my room."

Her sad tone was just about more than I could take. "You sure?" I called after her.

"Yes, Mother." She rolled her eyes and let out a breath.

"Well, I'll make you a smoothie and stick it in the fridge. Come get it whenever you're ready." I smiled, suddenly thankful for the break between us before Hannah's unhappiness rubbed off on me.

Before I could make fruit smoothies, I had to pay the babysitter. And greet the twins. I enjoyed being a stay-at-home mom and was grateful to be available for my three girls, but I liked my time away too—a chance to step into the big world and socialize with adults. So every Tuesday, I went out to lunch with my friend Sandra. Today I was away longer than usual since I had to take Hannah to her orthodontist appointment and pick up her glasses at the optometry office.

"Mommy!" Ava and Lily ran toward me when I entered the family room, leaving their coloring books and crayons splayed across the dining room table.

"How are my girls?" I dropped to my knees and grabbed my four-year-olds around their waists, hugging them tight. They were miracle babies, born six weeks early, but you'd never know it by their endless supply of energy. And intelligence. I wanted to put them in kindergarten early, but Jason chose to hold them back, saying there was plenty of time for them to be in school. I'm glad I listened. Kids are only little once.

Samantha, our twentysomething babysitter, stood and grabbed her purse. "I tried to clean up, but every time I put something away, they grabbed something else off the shelf."

My life story.

I reached into my purse for money and handed it to Samantha. "We'll work on that, right, girls?"

Ava and Lily nodded, appeasing me for the moment.

"Same time next week?" I asked Samantha, hoping nothing had changed in her busy college schedule.

"I'll be here. Bye, girls!" Samantha scooted toward the door—dodging baby dolls, puzzle pieces, books, and stuffed animals.

When she closed the door behind her, I motioned Ava and Lily toward the couch to have a heart-to-heart chat. "Hannah is sad today, and we need to cheer her up. Who wants to help me?"

They both raised their hands.

"Why is Hannah sad?" Lily asked.

How could I explain to my little girls what it's like to be in middle school?

Philippians 4:8 came to mind. "Fix your thoughts on what is true, and honorable, and right, and pure, and lovely, and admirable. Think about things that are excellent and worthy of praise" (NLT).

The verse was a good reminder. How many times had I dwelled on things that made me sad or anxious instead of things that were true and honorable, right and pure? All God's gifts were worthy of praise.

"We have to cheer Hannah up because she's thinking about things that make her sad instead of things she's grateful for—like trees with spring leaves, music, and fruit smoothies."

Ava smiled. "I like smoothies."

"Me too," I said. "But before we can make them, we need to clean up this mess."

Ava and Lily jumped to their feet, gathered toys, and put them back on the shelves or in the toy box. I watched my little munchkins work, relieving me from cleanup duty. At least for today.

Fifteen minutes later, Ava, Lily, and I gathered in the kitchen. We took turns dumping strawberries, yogurt, and orange juice into the blender, then mixing them up into Hannah's favorite drink. Before I poured the smoothies, the girls and I raced into the yard with a basket and picked anemones, azaleas, crabapple blooms, and a few sunflowers to create a beautiful spring bouquet. I placed the arrangement in the middle of the table next to a notecard with Hannah's name on it.

Next, we pulled up Hannah's Spotify account on the computer and blasted the music. Ava and Lily danced around the room, and I smiled, praising God for the gifts of my beautiful children.

But Hannah didn't join us.

Lord, please help her see all that is excellent and praiseworthy.

I poured the sweet pink liquid into glass cups, filled to the top, and set them on the table.

"Where's Hannah?" Lily asked.

Before I had a chance to answer, my tween girl entered the room. Her eyes were a little red and puffy behind her new frames, but she tipped her lips into a smile, showing the turquoise-colored bands around her new braces. "I love this song."

I tuned my ears to listen, but I didn't recognize the tune. Didn't matter. My daughter had said something positive!

Lily grabbed her sister's hand. "Are you still sad?"

I sucked in a breath, hoping Lily's question didn't catch

Hannah off guard, pushing her back to her depressed state and ruining the nice moment.

"No, I'm not," Hannah said.

"Oh, I'm so glad." I motioned for the girls to take a seat at the table to enjoy their smoothies. "Pretty soon you'll be in high school with gorgeous straight teeth, and in a few years you can get contacts."

Hannah furrowed her brows. "I wasn't sad because I have to wear glasses and braces. There are a lot of kids like me in middle school."

"Then why the cold shoulder today?"

"I found out Jacob likes Kaitlyn and wants to take her to the spring dance."

"Jacob Malloy, the boy you've had a crush on since fourth grade?"

"Yep." Hannah shrugged and took a sip of her strawberry smoothie. "But it's okay. I'd rather stay friends with Kaitlyn than worry about some guy who's never even noticed me."

Fix your thoughts on what is true and honorable. It appeared my daughter knew that lesson better than I did.

"That's admirable." I sat and took a sip of my smoothie. "You have a great attitude."

"Thanks." Hannah smiled and licked her lips. "And thank you for cheering me up. I love the smoothie, the music, and especially the flowers. They're … lovely."

Since when did Hannah use that word? I laughed. "You're very welcome."

Yes, all of God's gifts are worthy of praise.

Life Application

The world around us focuses on the things we think we need to make us happy instead of the things we value most. Instead of thinking about what is right and pure, our culture tells us to strive for a life that looks good to others.

It's difficult to teach our children about what is honorable and true when society points them in a different direction. Many times moms get caught in that trap too.

Second Corinthians 4:18 says, "We don't look at the troubles we can see now; rather, we fix our gaze on things that cannot be seen. For the things we see now will soon be gone, but the things we cannot see will last forever" (NLT).

When we focus on God and His gifts, our earthly troubles pale in comparison. As we walk the paths we've been given, our minds will be filled with all that is excellent and worthy of praise. And we will be at peace.

About the Author

Sherry Kyle is an award-winning author who writes novels for women, both contemporary and historical, as well as books for tween girls. Sherry is a graduate of Biola University and has been married to Douglas, her college sweetheart, for nearly thirty years. They have four almost-grown children and make their home on the coast of California. Visit Sherry on the web at sherrykyle.com.

3

Here with Us

by Nancy Ellen Hird

My house keys—where are they? I just had them. I give my purse another shake. Calm down, I tell myself. You'll get in—maybe not tonight, but …

I glance over my shoulder. My parents puff their way up my garden walk. I should have insisted they leave my luggage in the car.

I set down my carry-on and give full attention to key hunting in my purse. No luck.

"Matt," I call softly to an open upstairs window. "Can you come down and open the door?"

My husband does not appear. I consider yelling, but don't want to disturb the neighbors at this hour. In frustration I slap at my coat pocket. Ah! The jangle of keys.

"Matthew," I call out as I enter the house.

"We're up here," he stage whispers.

We? The word catches me off guard. For a moment I don't know whether to run toward it or away from it.

I drop everything. My purse spills open, and the remnants of my old life cartwheel around my feet. I step over the clutter and bolt up the stairs.

Matt is on the landing. In his arms he cradles a small pink bundle. How tiny a newborn is. My husband bends his dark head to her ear and whispers, "Mommy's here."

My breath catches. Tears fill my eyes as I put my arms out for the baby. I need to touch her, know she's real.

All the way home on the long flight from my business trip in London, I kept steeling myself for the worst. *It's going to fall through. I'll get home and find out the birth mother changed her mind.* The emptiness. The disappointment. I can't go through that. *Please, God. Please.*

The baby feels so light, and her skin is so red. Is she all right? She's rather funny looking. Is she going to be homely?

"So, Mom," I say, "what do you think? Cute, huh?" My mother will know if something's wrong. She's had lots of experience, even though it's been thirty-six years since she gave birth to me.

"Let me sit down and hold her."

Matt and I usher her and Dad into our bedroom. I glance around at the brass lamps, the antique four-poster bed, the blue wingback chairs. The room looks the same as when I left, yet it feels completely different. Maybe it's the baby bottle on the floor and the bassinet peeking out from behind the chair.

Mom sits in one of the wingbacks and coos to the infant.

I watch her finger the tiny hands and count the toes. She smiles—everything is fine.

I relax and close my eyes, suddenly very tired. I've been awake for two days straight, ever since we got the call from the agency. Packing my stuff from the company apartment in London, putting my work in order, making plane reservations—it's all catching up with me. I may not have gone through labor for this baby, but I have definitely labored for her.

"Kristin, we're going to leave now," Dad says. He sounds far away. I open my eyes and realize that I've fallen asleep standing against the door jamb.

"She's beautiful," Mom says, handing the baby to Matt.

I lie down on the bed. My husband kisses my forehead and lays the little one beside me. The sound of her breathing is sweet in my ear. I touch the soft blanket and then the even softer cheek. Such peace. Such joy.

Suddenly my stomach knots. *What if …?* I push down the fears. This baby will be ours forever. And yet I scoot away a little from her.

I awake at five thirty. Outside my bedroom window, the sky has gone from blue velvet to slate gray. But one corner of our room is soft gold. Matt has turned the table lamp on low. He sits in a chair next to it, feeding the baby. He smiles at me, a look of pure contentment. "What do you think about naming her Casey?"

"It's nice. But can we think about it some more?"

"What name did you have in mind?"

I shrug. "I don't know."

"What's wrong with Casey?"

"Nothing," I snap.

He looks like I punched him.

"I need a cup of coffee." I offer him a small smile and flee to the kitchen.

As I grab a mug off the shelf, my hand shakes. I bite my lip. In this cold half-light, I admit it. I'm not ready to name her. We just got her. Everything still feels too dreamlike, too fluid, too impermanent.

I grumble at the oak clock and pour myself a cup of coffee. I can't call anyone until eight. Well, maybe seven thirty. If I call Lisa at seven fifteen, she probably won't freak too much.

I sip the hot liquid and picture my older sister, sleeping in now that her last child has gone off to college. I won't know that experience for quite a while. I'm just beginning my journey.

Did we wait too long to stop trying to have a child naturally? I had no idea how lengthy the adoption process would be. But finally, after watching my nieces and nephews grow up, it's my turn.

A tentative feeling of excitement rises within me.

"Well, do I get to hold her, or are you going to hog her?" Lisa says, shooting Matt a teasing glare.

My husband grins. He's absolutely tickled with this child. He lays the baby in my sister's arms like she's a priceless jewel. Which, of course, she is.

"Hold her head," he admonishes.

I expect my sister to roll her eyes and tell him that she remembers how to treat a newborn. But she just smiles and lets him instruct her.

"Oh, what a sweetie," Lisa bubbles. She strokes the baby's cheek. "What's her name?"

"She doesn't have one yet," I say, a little too quickly. "We're trying out names to see which one fits her best."

Lisa nods. "Sounds good."

It does. Yet something nags at me.

The baby stirs. Her tiny lips begin to suck.

"She's waking up," Matt says. "I'll go get her a bottle."

I watch him leave, waiting for him to be out of earshot. Then I turn to my sister. "Lisa." I try to clear the lump from my throat. "The baby's mother—"

"Hey. You're the baby's mother."

I smile feebly. "The birth mother has six months to think about it before she has to sign the paperwork. She said she won't wait that long, but …" Old doubts die hard. "I don't think she'll take her back. I really don't." I say it firmly, more to convince myself than my sister.

Lisa studies me for a moment. Then she stares at the wall. I wish I could read her mind. But I'm having trouble understanding my own.

"Oh, Lisa, I can't stop thinking she's going to come and take her away. I don't know what I'd do if that happened. It would break Matt's heart, that's for sure."

Lisa pulls the baby closer to her chest. Her eyes are fierce, her mouth hard.

I can't help but grin. If anybody wants to take this baby, they'll have to fight me, Matt, and—won't they be sorry!—my sister.

Lisa's mouth softens and she looks at me evenly. I brace myself.

"If the birth mother did take her …"—she inhales a deep breath—"… you'd be able to handle it, because God would be with you. You'd be terribly sad, of course. It'd hurt. A lot." Her eyes mist. "A mother loves her kids so much it almost rips her apart to let them …" She looks away.

I gently squeeze her arm.

"Kristie, all kids go away eventually. It's part of the parenting deal. We only get to borrow them for a short time." She gazes tenderly at the baby and strokes the tiny fist. It opens, and the newborn wraps her little fingers around Lisa's big forefinger. My sister gives the infant a brilliant, triumphant smile. "But what an awesome privilege that borrowing time is."

After Lisa goes home, I wander into the living room. A stack of books for naming babies lies on one end of the coffee table. I sit on the couch at the opposite end and pull my knees up to my chin, still not ready to make that commitment.

Upstairs Matt starts singing. Is it a lullaby? Not really, but he makes it sound like one. I rock back and forth.

I recall sitting just like this—curled up on the couch, afraid to move—the night before my wedding. I almost called off the marriage. Sure am glad now that I didn't.

I uncurl and walk over to the books. Taking a deep breath, I pick up the one on top. I turn to the C's. We decided we definitely want a C name. I let my eyes roam a page.

One name jumps out at me. Cher. The book says it means "dear one." That fits her perfectly. She will be our dear one forever … whether she stays with us or not.

But oh God, please. Let her be here with us for a long, long time.

Life Application

Spending time with a child is a gift from God, whether you're a parent, a grandparent, an aunt or uncle, a teacher, a neighbor, or a foster parent. God uses children to teach us about Himself and about ourselves.

Scripture calls us the children of God, not the grown-ups of God. Like children, we are learners, not "knowers." We need lots of practice at life skills. And it's okay if we don't get something right the first time.

Being with a child can help us glimpse truth. Not because everything a child does is right, but because a child's ways are less complicated. Unvarnished. Children can also help us see the beauty and majesty in small things. They can slow us down to notice the sky in a puddle or experience the pleasure in a simple hello.

Of course, spending time with a child can also be exhausting, even troubling. Preparing meals, doing laundry, chauffeuring, settling quarrels, answering constant questions can all sap our strength and numb our minds. But even these experiences can be a blessing because we have to turn to God for power and wisdom. We don't have enough on our own. We need His love, gentleness, and patience to fill us up. Only then can it flow through us to others.

When we allow ourselves to be part of the life of a child, God gives us all the love we need.

About the Author

Nancy Ellen Hird is the mother of a grown daughter. She is also the team leader of Books 4 Christian Kids, http://nancy ellenhird.wordpress.com, a blog that recommends books that will uplift children. Her latest book, *I Get a Clue,* is a mystery novel for girls ages ten to thirteen.

4

Haiti's Song

by Deborah Raney

Sa Bo-Dié séré pou ou, lavalas pa poté-l alé.
(What God has laid up for you, the flood will not carry away.)
—Haitian proverb

Valerie Austin shifted in the cramped window seat and peered out over the murky blue-green waters of the Atlantic. As the Boeing 757 emerged from a bank of clouds, she thought she could make out the string of jade-colored Bahama islands where she was supposed to have spent her honeymoon.

The reservations in an elegant seaside hotel had long since been canceled, and the bed that awaited her party of one would likely be a concrete floor or, if she were lucky, a narrow cot.

Valerie trusted that someday she would be able to look back and be grateful she'd been dumped. But couldn't Will have left her before the invitations went out?

Despite the lousy timing, she realized that this humiliation was better than an unhappy marriage or eventual divorce. Still, it hurt. She had loved William Concannon, and she'd be lying if she claimed he hadn't broken her heart.

Tears, hot and stinging, welled behind her eyelids. She reached for her carry-on bag and found a tissue, then slipped her passport from the zippered pocket.

She opened the little blue book and read the sheet of scrap paper tucked inside. *Lespwa pou l'Avni Children's Home.* Some honeymoon destination. An orphanage on the outskirts of Port au Prince, Haiti. The name of the orphanage meant "hope for the future." Ironic when she thought about Will and the dreams she'd had for their future.

But that was exactly the problem. They were *her* dreams. It wasn't Will's fault he didn't share those dreams. From childhood, Valerie had only wanted one thing out of life. Children. A dozen of them.

But her twenties had flown by, and as her biological clock ticked frantically, her dream became a desperate prayer. *Please, God, I want a child. Just one child to love and to love me in return.* Surely that wasn't too much to ask.

And then Will came along, handsome and funny, and they shared a strong Christian faith. He seemed like the answer to her prayers.

Until the night she told him about her dream. She could still see that deer-in-the-headlights expression he'd seemed unable to erase from his chiseled features.

"You want … kids?"

"Well, of course. Who doesn't?"

His Adam's apple bobbed in his throat. "Um … *I* don't. It wouldn't be fair. How could we fit kids into our busy life?"

"But you love children! I've seen you with them."

He taught the junior high class in their church. He was great with those students, and they adored him in return.

"Well, sure," he'd said, brushing a strand of hair from her face. "Other people's kids. After they're past the rug-rat stage."

She pulled away, feeling numb.

Will took her hand and started talking about the dreams *he* had nurtured from childhood. "I want to travel the world, Val. There are still some mountains I haven't climbed. Oh, and I signed up for a parachuting class in the fall."

"But that's so dangerous."

"Since when have I ever shied away from danger?"

"Since you got engaged and realized it was time to grow up and be responsible?"

She'd tried to convince Will that fatherhood would be the greatest adventure he could imagine. But she couldn't quite persuade him that three a.m. feedings and changing dirty diapers would give him the same adrenaline rush as traversing the jungle canopy on a zip line.

She'd been almost relieved when Will called off the engagement. But she didn't think she could ever forgive him for denying her the only thing she'd ever really wanted from life.

Sighing, she smoothed the wrinkles from the casual cotton shift she wore. A dress of her own design, but a far cry from the four bridesmaids' dresses and the wardrobe she'd sewn for her honeymoon in the tropics.

She'd started sewing long before she met Will, ever since her first year of middle-school home economics, when she discovered how smoothly a sewing machine handled beneath her touch.

When she was sixteen she paid ten cents at a garage sale for a pattern. She sewed a frilly sundress, toddler size two, from lime-green gingham check, with a ruffled eyelet slip peeking from beneath the skirt. She spent a week's allowance on some tiny buttons shaped like lemons, limes, and oranges to trim the bodice.

That little dress was the first thing she put into her hope chest. Over the years she'd filled that trunk to overflowing with baby clothes. Boy things and girl things, all shapes and sizes. At night, in her room, while the rest of the house slept, she took each little outfit from the chest and pictured her babies wearing it. She prayed that God would bless her precious future children and keep them safe … and that she might have the privilege of praying with all of them to ask Jesus into their hearts.

Three days after Will broke their engagement, Valerie took everything out of the hope chest. She folded each outfit neatly and placed it in a cardboard box. She sealed the box that contained, literally, the last threads of her dream and mailed it to her sister in Chicago. Beth promised to give the clothes to her church's annual rummage sale.

Valerie shed a few tears that day. But now it was time to end the pity party.

Which was why, on this January morning that was sup-posed to have been her wedding day, she was on an airplane bound for Haiti. The orphanage her church sponsored was desperately in need of workers, and thanks to Will, she already had a passport, time off from her advertising job, and a plane ticket, which the airline had been kind enough to transfer—for a small fee.

A bell tone sounded and the captain came on to tell pas-sengers they were beginning the descent into Port au Prince.

Half an hour later, Valerie stepped onto the streets of the city. Her nostrils flared at the strange mingling of frying fish, exhaust fumes, garbage, and sewage.

She held a tissue to her nose and shaded her eyes, search-ing the crowd for the faces of Pastor and Madame Greene, the missionaries from the orphanage. There they were! Their silver heads and fair skin stood out like beacons amid the sea of ebony faces that swarmed outside the airport's metal fence. She waved, and they motioned for her to go to a gate a few yards away.

Once outside, she was instantly surrounded by children, mostly boys. Snow-white teeth grinned up at her from shiny black faces. They all shouted at once in their thick Creole accent, "Madame, one dollar please?"

Pastor Greene scolded the children with authority in his voice that belied his age. Stretching over the heads of the young beggars, he reached for her hand and smiled. "You must be Valerie," he shouted over the din.

"Yes." The word was scarcely off her lips before Madame

Nolan—as the Haitians called Pastor Greene's wife—plowed through the crowd and pulled Valerie into a bear hug that nearly knocked the wind out of her.

After loading her bags into an old van, Pastor Greene navigated the narrow streets of Port au Prince, weaving in and out of traffic, honking, and dodging automobiles that seemed not to care which side of the street they used. A few miles into the breathtaking ride—after they almost ran down a teenage boy balancing a wheelbarrow filled with cinder blocks—Valerie considered e-mailing Will to tell him she'd discovered an adrenaline rush unlike anything he'd ever experienced.

At the orphanage, a week flew by in a whirlwind, and Valerie scarcely gave William Concannon a thought. There wasn't time to think! Pastor Greene and Madame Nolan kept her busy with a list so varied she never knew from one moment to the next if she would be slicing lemons, painting cement blocks, or changing diapers. And she truly loved every minute of it.

Two days before she was to fly back home, she lay on her cot in the dark, feeling oddly unsettled. Sleep eluded her.

Outside her window she heard the traffic on the streets of Port au Prince, and in the distance the haunting drums of the village witch doctors. It made her shudder to think of the spiritual darkness that covered this land. What would happen when the Greenes could no longer manage the orphanage? They'd celebrated Pastor Greene's sixty-ninth birthday last week. He couldn't possibly have enough years left to see the smallest children safely into the world outside the gates. Especially with more coming all the time.

Tears rolling down her cheeks, she whispered into the darkness, "Oh, Father, give these precious saints as many years as they need. Bless these babies. And Lord, I know my problems are petty by comparison, but when I get home, please show me what You want me to do with my life."

She finally slept. The next morning, when she stepped into the sunny courtyard, she spotted Jacquette, a two-year-old, playing by herself in the shade of a courtyard wall. Squatting on lean haunches, the toddler scratched intently in the dirt with a stick.

Drawn by a magnetic pull she seemed powerless to resist, Valerie took a step closer. She heard Jacquette singing in her sweet, high voice. The words were Creole, but Valerie recognized the melody.

"*Mwen konnen Jezu renmenm', Se Bib la ki di mwen sa.*" Jesus loves me, this I know.

Valerie smiled, totally taken with this little ebony-faced beauty. When she was still a few feet away, Jacquette looked up at her and smiled broadly. She rose gracefully from her haunches and held out her stick to Valerie, jet-black eyes sparkling.

Valerie reached to take her offering, but as the little girl toddled forward into the sunlight, Valerie's breath caught. Surely she was imagining things! She dropped to her knees in front of the girl, accepting the stick from her pudgy hands.

Jacquette swayed, shyly fingering the skirt of her dress—her lime-green gingham-check dress with its white eyelet underskirt. She poked at a button on her bodice, then looked up at Valerie, beaming. "*Sitro*," she said proudly. The Creole word for lemon.

It wasn't possible! Yet there—right in front of her, modeled by this round-cheeked, cornrowed angel—was the very dress Valerie had sewn when she was sixteen! The dress with its buttons shaped like lemons and limes and oranges. The one she'd shipped off to a rummage sale an ocean away only weeks ago.

How had it ended up here? Then she remembered her sister telling her that an old woman had come in and snapped up the clothes for some charity.

But there were thousands of charities in the world, dozens of orphanages in Haiti alone.

Pastor Greene rang the bell signaling time for chapel. Her mind still racing, Valerie scooped Jacquette into her arms and went to help the older girls herd the little ones into the sanctuary.

She hummed the Creole choruses with her eyes closed, soaking in the rich harmonies of this rapturous children's choir, turning over in her mind again and again what had just taken place.

When it was time for devotions, she went to the back of the room to help quiet the younger children, who were growing restless. Valerie pulled Jacquette and another toddler onto her lap. Resting her chin between their two dark heads, she looked around at dozens of children wiggling in their seats.

And then she saw it.

Two rows in front of her, Henri wore a brown-and-green plaid shirt sewn from fabric left over from a jumper Valerie had sewn in tenth grade. Down the row from him, little Marie-Andrée wore a sleeveless shift of silky flocked magenta.

Valerie had ripped the seams of that dress more times than she cared to remember, trying to keep the fabric from puckering.

Her eyes roamed up and down the rows, and everywhere she looked were little motherless Haitian children wearing the clothes she'd made for her babies.

Madame Nolan's voice droned pleasantly in the background, and the children squirmed in Valerie's lap, but she and the Lord may as well have been alone together in that little chapel. His voice wasn't audible. Instead it was the still, small whisper she'd come to learn so intimately over these past few weeks.

Remember that request you put in for a dozen children? Valerie was sure God was smiling. *Remember those babies you prayed for so faithfully when you were a little girl yourself?*

Her throat closed up and she choked back tears of joy. She knew in that moment—more clearly than she'd ever known anything in her life—that she was home.

Valerie looked around the room and knew she was looking at her children—holding two of them on her lap. These were the babies she'd longed for and prayed for and waited not so patiently for, for almost three decades.

And it occurred to her that answers to prayer are even sweeter when you've been waiting for them your whole life.

Life Application

Probably more often than not, God answers our prayers and makes our dreams come true in very different ways than we imagine or would choose for ourselves. We may not realize it right way, perhaps not even until years later, but almost always—if we are following God's Word—we will realize that His answers to prayer and His fulfillment of our dreams are better than anything we could have planned.

Sometimes God doesn't answer our prayers or fulfill our dreams. But that's a good thing too. He knows us much better than we know ourselves. He also knows our future—which, if we knew, may change what we think is best for us.

Psalm 37:4 says, "Delight yourself also in the Lord, and He shall give you the desires of your heart" (NKJV). When we truly delight ourselves in the Lord, we will allow Him to exchange our desires for the dreams He wishes to fulfill in our lives. And there's nothing more satisfying than being in the very center of His will.

About the Author

Deborah Raney's first novel, *A Vow to Cherish*, inspired the World Wide Pictures film of the same title and launched Deb's writing career. Twenty years, thirty books, and numerous awards later, she's still creating stories that touch hearts and lives. She and her husband, Ken, recently traded small-town life in Kansas for life in the city of Wichita. They love traveling to visit their four grown children and five grandchildren (and still counting!), who all live much too far away.

Distant as the Horizon

by Kara Swanson

The water wrapped softly around her, less painful now due to the numbing cold. Light filtered downward, starlets catching their reflection in the bubbles that rose from her sinking body.

Tendrils of black hair brushed against her as she ran a gentle hand across her bulging middle. There were so many reasons she wished she could reach the surface—if not for herself, then for her child. But she was too weak, the water too frigid.

Instead, she resigned to be slowly gathered into the welcoming arms of death, a place where the cold couldn't catch her. Where she could breathe.

Danae jolted back into reality, blinded by the sun and acutely aware of a sticky substance clinging to her fingertips. Blinking, she realized that pools of aqua paint were spilling down her hands. She'd been daydreaming. Again. Watching her own mother drown moments before giving birth to her. After playing the story so often in her head, imagining every grotesque detail, it had become a habit.

Not that Danae would complain. Those fantasies were the only time she saw her mother.

Using the rag lying haphazardly on her easel, Danae scrubbed the paint from her hands and examined the sprawling image on her canvas, hoping she hadn't ruined the seascape when she drifted off

"Get a grip, girl," she muttered, trying to calm her shaking hands and whisk away the gloom that haunted her mother's memory. She dabbed more paint onto a brush and scanned the horizon. Pale sand spread out around her, fading into dark, craggy rock. Seawater pooled in the recesses of the granite, discolored by the plant life thriving within. To her right, a long pier stretched out from the shore, reaching toward the ocean. Waves churned beneath it, slamming into the rocks and the wooden pylons with a spray of whitewash.

The beach was uninhabited except for a young mother perched on a dry patch of rock, one giggling child in her lap and another bent over a tide pool. Thankfully, they were several feet from Danae. She wasn't so great with kids. Or parents. Or people in general.

Danae glanced back at the rippling ocean. It was beautiful and dangerous—two things that drew her. In spite of the harsh memories it brought, she still felt a grudging bond with the sea. These sunlit beaches and crashing waves were the only place she truly felt close to her mom.

With deft brush strokes, she layered the rim of ocean at the edge of her painting, adding a light swath of white for sea foam. Soft laughter wafted her way from the little family playing by the pier. One of the children was just a baby, the other a rambunctious toddler.

"Guess it'd be too much to ask for some peace," Danae muttered, turning to the tall lifeguard station set near the water's edge. A faded sign warned, "NO LIFEGUARD ON DUTY." Tuesday was Ian's day off.

With a sigh, Danae went back to painting, trying not to think about the tenderness that lit the mother's face. A gentleness she'd never seen in her own mom's eyes.

Danae had never seen her face at all. Only her grave.

By the time the doctors had managed to take Danae from her mother's body, she was already gone. Danae had lived, while her mom had died. The guilt would never fade.

Yet for some reason, Danae loved painting the very ocean that had taken her mother eighteen years ago.

Her thoughts were interrupted by the sound of desperate screaming. Spinning, she found the woman standing near the shoreline, baby clutched in her arms, pointing toward the pier and shouting incoherently.

A tiny blonde head bobbed in the water by one of the pylons. In a matter of minutes the next set of waves would crush the toddler.

Danae ran past the frantic mother and into the water. Soon the salty mire was up to her knees.

"Get Lace!" the mother wailed. "Don't let my baby die!"

A wave dragged the child underwater. Danae swam through the breakers and grasped her arm. Tears poured from Lace's big, frightened eyes, and a choking cry wracked her body. Her terror sent Danae's heart racing.

Coughing to fight back the swelling salt water that was trying to force its way into her mouth, Danae kicked hard to keep Lace above the churning water.

The current drew them nearly to the end of the pier, in water so deep that Danae's toes couldn't touch the bottom. Pounding waves came one after another, creating a mountain of whitewash that thundered all around them.

They were about to drown.

Panic sent chills through Danae's frenzied mind. She opened her mouth to scream. Suddenly, two tiny hands wrapped around her neck and a wet cheek pressed against hers. The tiny life clinging to her was depending on her strength for her very survival. Danae was not going to let her down.

Energized, she forced herself to keep fighting the raging waters. "Don't worry, Lace!" she yelled above the whitewash that drove her toward an outcropping of rocks. "I'm going to keep you safe." *No matter what.*

A few feet from shore, another current wrapped itself around their bodies, pulling them toward one of the pylons. When her shoulder rammed into it, Danae clamped her jaws shut, stifling a scream. A sickening crunch told her she'd broken something, but she was numb to any pain. Forcing her body into motion again, she kicked against the wood, using the bit of speed to launch herself toward the shoreline.

A blur of orange at the edge of her clouded vision caught her attention. Throat raw from the salt and eyes aching, she focused on that amber spot, watching it morph into a red-headed young man paddling a rescue board.

Ian!

He reached them within a few seconds.

Danae grabbed his float with one hand. "Take the kid first." She choked out, then clenched her eyes shut as another wave rocked them, salty brine spraying her face. Ian took Lace from her arms and settled the trembling little one onto the board. Next, he reached out with his free hand and helped Danae get a good grip on the device.

Together, they paddled over the waves to Lace's mother. Tears rolled down the woman's face when they reached the shore and placed the child in her arms.

Ian examined Lace, cleaning and wrapping her scrapes, while the toddler's mother hugged and thanked Danae a million times. After a few seconds, Danae squirmed out of the woman's embrace and returned to her art supplies.

When he finished with Lace, Ian crossed the beach to Danae and insisted that she let him look at her bruised shoulder. She settled on the warm sand and he gently prodded her arm.

"I can't believe you did that. You almost drowned."

"There was no one else around. I couldn't just let her die."

His eyes flashed at her. "You were willing to risk your life for a kid you don't even know?"

Her gaze drifted to Lace's mother, who held the toddler firmly in her arms as she packed the family's things. The blonde-fringed face stared at Danae, and the tiniest of smiles parted her rosebud lips.

"I guess I was."

Ian shook his head, opening his first-aid kit and taking out a tube of salve.

I was willing to die for a child who was practically a stranger. How much more would my own mother have been willing to die for me? What if she gladly gave her life to save mine?

Danae stood suddenly, knocking Ian backward. He said something, but she didn't hear his words. She trudged toward the water lapping at the edge of a twisted rock.

A deep breath expanded her chest as her gaze traced the rolling hues of the ocean, her artist eye picking out the lilting shades of blue.

For as long as she could remember, Danae had battled a weight far stronger than any wave. These rippling waters held so much significance. Life. Death. Joy. Fear. A deadly beauty. But there was one emotion the sea no longer held for her: guilt. That had been washed from Danae's soul and was as distant as the horizon.

Finally, she could breathe.

Life Application

Most of us suffer from an acute sense of guilt at some point in our lives. It can stem from many things, but always ends with lowered expectations and a tarnished view of ourselves. Guilt shackles our joy and changes our perception of the people around us. Yet, as children of God, we should not let a sense of failure control us. Our weaknesses should make His mercy shine even brighter.

Just as Danae and her mother were willing to give their lives for another out of love, Jesus sacrificed Himself for us. His love has washed our guilt away and given us a new chance to live in His joy.

"He will again have compassion on us. … You will cast all our sins into the depths of the sea" (Micah 7:19 ESV).

About the Author

Kara Swanson was raised in the jungle with her missionary family. She published her first book at sixteen, a fantasy novel called *Pearl of Merlydia,* which is available on Kindle and in paperback. Kara won the Most Promising Teen Writer Award at the 2015 Mount Hermon Christian Writers' Conference.

6

A Long Way from Monroe High

by Julie-Allyson Ieron

The magazines in the waiting room were so tattered that Courtney Davidson half expected to flip a page and see some 1970s Virginia Slims model pointing a finger at her to declare, "You've come a long way, baby." *Yeah, a long way.* She couldn't stifle a shiver. *From strutting across the stage in a purple-and-gold doctoral hood to … this.*

A scrub-clad twentysomething with fuchsia hair and black nails appeared in the dark doorway. "Ms. Davidson, the group will be meeting in the conference room." She gestured toward the third door on the left. "You're a bit early. But you can wait there for the others."

Courtney dropped the magazine and mumbled, "It's *Dr.* Davidson. Not *Miz.*" She'd invested five years of her life into earning the title Doctor of Ministry—she deserved a bit of respect. But she was beginning to wonder if she'd paid too great a cost for a degree she'd now have to shelve for months—maybe years.

Courtney made her way to the empty conference room and chose a seat. She hadn't expected this month to be an easy adjustment, moving back into her mom's house after spending a year's residency on campus completing coursework and preparing her dissertation. She knew the transition from academia to her new job as the county's fire-and-rescue chaplain would be a shock to her system. It was one thing to learn about ministry in class, but another to actually do it under real life-and-death conditions.

But her adjustment went into hyperdrive two weeks ago when she returned from a firehouse Bible study to find her mother sprawled on the bathroom floor. She'd instantly gone into professional mode: assess the situation, call for an ambulance, check the pulse, clear a path for the EMTs' arrival. All while speaking soothing words to Mom—who might be able to hear her voice, even though she was unconscious.

Courtney had nearly cried when she opened the door for the EMTs and recognized Paul, who had been at her Bible study session.

When he asked if her mother had any known medical conditions, Courtney muttered, "Not that I know of." Mom took her privacy to the extreme, especially when it came to her health.

At the hospital, the ER physician told Courtney her mother had broken bones, cuts, and bruises that would require months of rehab. And tests indicated the cause of the fall was "diabetic hyperosmolar syndrome"—a diabetic coma brought on by Mom's perilously high blood-sugar level.

Courtney had known nothing about her mother's diabetes until that moment. Apparently, Mom hadn't wanted to worry her during her residency. Didn't do anything about it herself, either. She hadn't been following the prescribed diet, taking her meds, or following up with the endocrinologist.

All that was about to change. Courtney was going to learn how to keep her mother's diabetes under control. That is, if anyone besides her showed up for this meeting.

Soon others filed into the conference room until nearly every chair was taken. Courtney met their glances with a smile and a nod, snapping back into her professional persona. Assured. Calm. Comforting to others.

Inside, though, she felt pretty much the opposite. *What if I can't handle Mom's diabetes? What if I mix up the meds or feed her something wrong? What if I'm not cut out to give her shots? She's always cared for me. What if I can't take care of her?*

When the black-nailed nurse shut the door and took her place at the white board, Courtney cringed. *What could I possibly learn from her? She's young enough to be my daughter, if I had one.*

The conference room door opened again, and one more attendee clamored in. "Sorry I'm late." He plopped down in the only remaining empty seat—next to Courtney.

Derrick James? From senior-year homeroom? Nah, couldn't be.

As the lecture began, Courtney became so engrossed with taking notes that she forgot all about the guy next to her. Food groups, proteins, and low-glycemic foods. How to measure and chart blood sugar. How to tell if a spike warranted an emergency trip to the hospital or a call to the doctor. Despite her unorthodox appearance, nail girl was a skilled communicator.

When she demonstrated how to use an insulin pen, Courtney breathed a sigh of relief. Administering shots wasn't as complicated as she'd anticipated. "It's really that easy?" she blurted out.

"Yeah. I've been doing it for my daughter for a couple of weeks now." The voice that came from beside her was rich and masculine. She turned to look and met the same gray-green eyes that had drawn her in all those years ago. He winked and grinned.

Courtney resisted the urge to glance at his left ring finger.

After the two-hour class ended, Courtney felt a tap on her shoulder. "HR402, right? James Monroe High?"

Act nonchalant. "Derrick! My goodness—it has been a while."

"I read that you were back in town."

"Local paper, huh? Hard to go unnoticed in such a small place."

"What're you doing in this class? Did you get diagnosed with Type Two?"

"No, Mom did. She also had an accident at home, so I'm taking a leave of absence from my job to help her get her strength back."

"I remember your mother. I hope she'll be okay."

"Me too. Thanks. So, you have a daughter?"

"Yeah. She's five. Type One. Her momma had it too. I lost her three years ago." He swiped his iPhone and turned it toward Courtney. The screen revealed two sweet faces—a lovely young woman and a toddler, a miniature image of the woman. "Cindy and Layla."

"I'm so sorry for your loss. How do you handle being both mother and father?"

"My mom and Cindy's mom help a lot. Layla loves her grandmothers, and they both adore her." He swiped to a more recent picture of the tot. "Do you have kids?"

"No. I've been too busy earning a seminary degree to look for a husband."

His eyebrow rose. "Really? All those eligible seminarians must have been blind." Derrick grinned.

She chuckled. "You always were good at raising my spirits."

Courtney looked around and realized they were the only ones left in the conference room. "Guess we'd better go." Not that she wanted to.

"Would you like to continue getting reacquainted over coffee or something?"

She smiled. "Yeah. I'd like that."

Life Application

Courtney set aside her dreams for her education, her goals to care for her mother, her preconceptions to learn from someone who seemed less accomplished, and her past disappointments for a renewed friendship. Life may give us similar opportunities.

As our parents pass through the various seasons of life, our understanding of the fifth commandment expands exponentially. Honoring them may mean setting aside our goals so Mom or Dad can receive the best care, comfort, and compassion—and the best of our energies. As we sit in cancer wards or wait for heart surgeries, our plans play second-fiddle to their needs. Our mothers have done this for us over the years; now it's our turn.

It's natural to feel that our sacrifices are too great to bear. But as we offer our parents acts of tender care, we're honoring God. I love the promise that God "will not forget how … you have shown your love to him by caring for other believers" (Hebrews 6:10 NLT). Caring, especially for our moms, is something God will remember. Similarly, Paul assures us, "Nothing you do for the Lord is ever useless" (1 Corinthians 15:58 NLT).

We can pour our energies into selfless choices with confidence, because we're in the employ of the one who notices, places value on our service, and never forgets.

About the Author

Julie-Allyson Ieron, author of thirty-seven books, recently published a fiction/nonfiction hybrid, *The GOD Interviews*. She writes Christian living, Bible studies, books about caregiving, and devotionals. After caring for her father and grandmother until their passing, Julie and her mother, Joy, have expanded their reach through worship leadership alongside the chaplain of a senior village.

7

The Real Mother

by Ann Tatlock

For eighteen years she had known this day would come. Why, then, did she suddenly feel so unprepared?

Judy Forrester stood at the front window, watching for the one car that would not pass by the house, but would slow down and pull into the drive. She was waiting for Della Gladstone, a woman she hadn't seen since … well, since Katie was born.

With each passing car, her heart jumped. She clasped her hands together and held them to her chest. She didn't say the words out loud, but they hung heavy in her mind: *God, give me strength.*

In the dining room, the table was set for tea: fine china, linen napkins, the antique floral teacups. Finger sandwiches waited in the fridge. A variety of fresh-baked cookies sat neatly arranged on a serving tray. Katie had done everything should could think of to impress her visitor.

She now sat on the couch in the living room, looking through a stack of photo albums. Judy had put them together over the years, beginning on the day she brought Katie home from the hospital.

The private adoption had been arranged by relatives when unmarried seventeen-year-old Della found herself pregnant. Judy and Della were distant cousins; Judy had never even met her. But more than anything in the world, she and David had wanted a baby. The agreement was that Judy would keep Della updated on the child's progress through letters. Della wouldn't see her until she turned eighteen. And only if Katie wanted to meet her.

Last week, Katie expressed a desire to meet her "real mother."

"I'm your real mother," Judy had said.

Katie had smiled apologetically. "Well, you know what I mean."

She did. All too well.

"I'm really scared, Mom."

Judy turned from the window to meet Katie's gaze. Her daughter looked up at her from the couch. With dark hair and blue eyes, she had grown into a beautiful young woman. "Of course you are, honey. That's only natural."

"What if she doesn't like me?"

Judy shook her head. "She'll love you. She won't be able to help it."

Katie managed a small, uncertain smile. "I hope I'm doing the right thing."

Tears pushed at the backs of Judy's eyes. "Of course you are."

Katie nodded and returned her attention to the photo album in her lap.

Judy understood why Katie wanted to meet the woman who had given birth to her. But she didn't like it. Would the connection undermine the bond she had so carefully built over the whole of Katie's lifetime? She had lost David eleven years ago. Would she lose her only child now too?

"Hey, I remember this." Katie tapped an index finger on one of the photos. "I fell off the swing and had to get stitches in my head."

Judy laughed. "You screamed so loud my ears rang for hours."

Katie turned a page. "Oh, and there's Mr. Betterbear when I first got him."

"Mr. Betterbear?"

"The night I hurt myself, Daddy ran out and bought me this teddy bear, and you sewed a line of stitches in his head to match mine."

"I remember." Judy glanced at the clock on the wall. Della was late. Probably got lost trying to find the house.

Katie picked up another photo album. She had insisted that all thirteen albums be at the ready so she could show her birth mother the entire sequence of her growing-up years. It would take hours to look through those photos. Especially if they shared all the stories behind them.

Ten minutes passed. Then fifteen. Judy's hands squeezed together until her fingers hurt.

After relinquishing her first child, Della had gone on to get married and have three more kids. She didn't need Katie—not the way Judy did. Oh, why had she agreed to this meeting when the adoption papers were drawn up?

"I haven't seen these pictures in years," Katie said. "I'd almost forgotten some of this stuff."

Katie seemed mesmerized by the photos. She ran her hands over them, touching each one gently. At one point, she frowned. "Whatever happened to this rocking chair?"

Judy forced herself to leave the window and look over Katie's shoulder at the picture. The tranquil scene of mother and child pierced her heart. "It's in the attic. You didn't want it in your room anymore when we got you the new bedroom set for your thirteenth birthday."

Katie nodded. "You used to sit in it beside my bed every night, reading books, telling me stories."

"Convincing you to go to sleep was never easy. You used to talk about the funniest things just to keep me there."

"I did? Like what?"

Judy thought a moment. "One time you asked, 'Mommy, when I'm grown up, will you be little so I can take care of you?' I said, 'That's a nice thought, honey. But when you're grown up, I will just be old.'"

They laughed.

Outside in the street, a car slowed. Judy rushed back to the window.

"Is it her?" Katie asked.

The car turned into the drive. Judy's knees felt weak.

"Mom?"

"Yes, honey." She turned.

Katie's eyes glistened. "Whatever happens today, I want you to know. You're the best mom ever."

Judy couldn't speak.

Outside, a car door slammed.

Katie rose from the couch. Judy opened her arms and her daughter fell into them. They held each other tight.

When the doorbell rang, Katie drew back and wiped her eyes with the back of her hand. "I'll let her in."

Judy touched her daughter's face. "I'll start the water for tea."

Moving to the kitchen, Judy smiled as she heard the front door open. She would make the tea and serve the finger sand-wiches for Della Gladstone's visit. Afterward she and Katie would clean up the kitchen, put the photographs away, and maybe make some popcorn and watch an old movie together before calling it a day.

No longer afraid, she put the teapot on the stove, then went to join the reunion in the hall.

Life Application

God is the ultimate adoptive parent. He didn't have to accept any of us as His children, but He chose to make us His own because He loves us. Romans 8:15–16 tells us, "You received the Spirit of adoption by whom we cry out, 'Abba, Father.' The Spirit Himself bears witness with our spirit that we are children of God" (NKJV). Through our physical birth, we are born into sin and our hearts belong to the world. But God gives us the opportunity to be "born again" by trusting in the sacrifice of Jesus to cleanse us of sin. We then belong to a new family, the family of God. We can come to God without fear and call Him Daddy.

We never have to question whether or not we belong to God. There is no greater love than that of the heavenly Father for His child. The bond is unbreakable. His love is unchangeable. All He asks is that we love Him in return.

About the Author

Ann Tatlock is a novelist and children's book author. Her newest novel, *Once Beyond a Time*, was published in December 2014 by Heritage Beacon Fiction/LPC. Her books have received numerous awards, including the Christy, the Selah, and the Midwest Book Award. Her daughter, Laura, was adopted from China in 1998. Ann lives with her family in western North Carolina. Visit her website at anntatlock.com.

8

Blustery, Beautiful Love

by Cindy Woodsmall

Becca turned off the shower, opened the curtain, and grabbed a towel. Thick steam swirled, clinging to the mirror. The weeks of angry words between her and her mother hung in the air like the mist from the hot shower. Becca was seventeen years old, the youngest of nine children, and her Mamm had simply forgotten what it was like to be young.

After getting dressed, Becca released her damp hair from its bun, combed it, and pinned it up again. She gazed at her image in the now-clear mirror. Despite the type of cape dress she'd worn her whole life, she liked the womanly figure she saw in her reflection. She wasn't a child anymore. But as good as that felt, nothing compared to her burning desire to have fun.

Before opening the bathroom door, she paused, drew in a deep breath, and prepared herself to go yet another round with her parents about the party tonight. Late-afternoon sunshine spilled from the windows at each end of the hallway, and rays of light danced across the old wood floor, mixing with the long shadows of autumn.

Becca eased down the stairs, hoping to avoid seeing her mother. When the last step creaked, Mamm looked up from the ironing board.

"Where's Daed?" Becca asked.

"Helping your uncle with the evening milking."

She breathed a sigh of relief. If another quarrel erupted, at least it would only be with one parent.

Mamm set the flat of the pressing iron on the wood-burning stove. Without looking at Becca, she held out a freshly ironed prayer Kapp. "I'm weary of arguing. The truth is, I don't know what else to say to you."

For a woman at a loss for words, her Mamm had said a lot in those two sentences. She wanted her daughter to come home directly after the singing, like she used to do.

Becca took the Kapp, biting back the harsh words that sprang to her mind.

Mamm sighed, her forehead furrowed. "There will be a price to pay for dabbling in worldly ways."

She'd heard this lecture until she was sick of it. "Good job of saying nothing else, Mamm. How long did that resolve last? Sixty seconds?"

"I'm just worried about you."

"You're always worried about something. At least let me have some fun while you're wringing your hands over me."

"But you're getting in deeper and deeper. Can't you see that? You don't understand what can become of these—"

"I do understand! Better than you think. You're being selfish. Admit it. This isn't just about me. You're worried over what your friends will think if they find out I go to parties. And you're so filled with fear, you can't let me enjoy some freedom!"

Mamm's cheeks flushed red. She opened her mouth to say something, but turned and left the room.

Good. Maybe Becca's ride to the singing would arrive before her mother got a second wind and returned to argue some more.

Becca went to the sewing machine and pulled a couple of pieces of double-sided tape off its holder. She moved to a nearby mirror, stuck the tape on the inside brim of her prayer Kapp, put it on, and pressed it against her hair. Like most Amish girls her age, Becca dressed according to tradition when in her parents' home. After the church-sponsored singing, she would let her hair down and change into more flattering Englisch clothes.

Becca enjoyed the singings—except that they were chaperoned, and the girls sat on one side of the room and the boys on the other, just like at Sunday meetings. After the last song, guys and girls were allowed to mingle while the chaperones served refreshments. As the group dispersed, a lot of the guys drove the goody-two-shoes girls home by horse and buggy. Until a few months ago, Becca was in that category. Then she dared to accept an invitation to join a group of youth who, after the singing, went to a "hangout"—an out-of-the-way cabin or shed—to party.

With eight older siblings, Becca had heard about hangouts since she was young. As far as she knew, her siblings had never attended such a party. They behaved appropriately. But Becca's youth would be gone in the blink of an eye. She'd watched her siblings go from teens to work-laden adults almost overnight. Soon after, they got married, had babies, and started acting just like Becca's parents: all work and zero fun.

No thanks!

Becca loved the loud music that blasted from battery-powered Englisch devices. She enjoyed fruity drinks laced with alcohol. And if things went really well tonight, she would meet a guy who was fun to talk to and dance with, and he'd give her a kiss that would make her head spin long after the alcohol wore off.

Some girls her age went too far—way beyond dancing and kissing. Her Mamm would call Becca's behavior a slippery slope—if she actually knew what her daughter was doing. But what *couldn't* be called a slippery slope? Becca wasn't stupid. She wouldn't do anything too foolish.

As she packed a small makeup bag, guilt nibbled at her. What did God think of her newfound self-indulgence? Or about her fighting with her parents? Remorse grew heavier. All she wanted was to have a good time. Why did Mamm resist that so much that Becca had to wage war in order to get even a little bit of wiggle room?

Through the window, Becca saw her cousin arrive in a horse-drawn carriage. She grabbed her purse and hurried out the door.

A kerosene lantern flickered as Ruth sorted through boxes in the attic. After her daughter left, she'd collapsed onto the couch, sobbing and praying. Then an idea came to her—to find an old pair of roller skates. If Becca saw them, maybe she'd remember …

Ruth had been searching for the skates for hours. Her husband had helped for a while, but he went to bed long ago.

Finally! At the bottom of a huge container lay a small, tattered white box. Memories of Becca learning to skate flooded Ruth's mind as she pulled it out. Tears welled. She loved her daughter so much. But a parent's feelings for a child weren't usually returned, at least not in the adolescent years. The mother-daughter bond was unbreakable to a mom, but easily broken to a teen.

Ruth had raised eight children. They all had homes of their own now. Becca was the last of the brood, and maybe the most difficult. But each child had gone through a tough year, both in their attitudes and in their decisions. For Becca, that season was now.

If Ruth had learned anything in her thirty-three years of raising children, it was that, to a teenager, parents are the enemy.

Ruth didn't know where Becca went after the singings. Or what she did there. Or what her actions might lead to. If the church didn't approve of Amish teens being allowed to "fellowship" with one another, Ruth would have refused to let her daughter leave the house. But that wasn't the Amish way. Maybe it wasn't God's way either. What did she know? Only that she felt an overwhelming desire to keep her youngest daughter from ruining her life.

Did all young people have to learn lessons the hard way? Nothing helped a child mature more than a little life experience.

Book learning could only go so far, even if the book was the Bible. Without the need to forgive someone, the Scripture passages exhorting people to forgive wouldn't really make sense.

Ruth took the box of roller skates downstairs, praying with every step for the right words to say to her daughter. She used a damp cloth to wipe years of dust off the white-and-pink leather. After lining the box with purple tissue paper, she put the skates back inside. She then got out the prettiest wrapping paper they owned, the shiny silver one used for wedding presents, and covered the box in it. After putting on a bow, she blew out the kerosene lamp and went to the couch in the living room to wait.

A moonbeam stretched across the wall, revealing the hands on the clock. When they reached 12:32, Ruth's anger began to stir again. Becca knew better than to stay out this late. That girl had grit, resolve, and nerves of steel. Those traits could be powerful if used for God. But right now she was using them to fight for the wrong things.

At 1:06 Ruth finally heard the clip-clop of horse's hooves against the concrete driveway. A few moments later, the back door creaked open. Trying to temper her wrath, Ruth walked through the dark house toward the back door, carrying the box.

Becca stopped cold when she saw her mother. "I didn't mean to be so late."

Standing in the dimly lit kitchen, Ruth held out the gift toward her. "I wrapped up an old item, like we used to do when you were young." Moonlight reflected on the shiny silver paper.

Becca didn't budge.

Ruth pulled a box of matches from her apron pocket and passed it to her daughter. "Why don't you light a lantern?"

Without an argument, Becca went to the kitchen table and put a burning match to the wick of a lamp.

Ruth closed the gap between them and held out the gift again. "Regardless of how I may sound to you, I love you just as much today as when you were my little angel."

Becca's eyes held disbelief, but she accepted the gift, carefully removed the paper, and opened the lid. "My skates." She lifted them out of the box. "The first *new* thing I ever owned."

Ruth shrugged. "That's the problem with being the ninth child."

"Was I seven years old?"

"Five."

She hugged the skates to her chest. "Oh, how I loved these." Becca laughed. "Do you remember skating with me the day I got them?"

"Vividly." Ruth had used her oldest son's skates, and her feet had blisters for a week afterward. But a mom of nine rarely had time with only one child, and spending the beautiful, blustery fall day skating with wide-open arms and letting the wind rush across her skin was something she'd never forget. "Do you remember what happened the next day?"

Becca ran her fingers over the wheels, making them spin. "*Ya*," she whispered.

Were those tears in her eyes?

She played with the shoestrings on the skates. "I figured I knew how to skate well enough to do it on the road."

Their long driveway was made of smooth concrete, but that wasn't enough for Becca. She had begged and pleaded for permission to skate down their street—a busy, narrow road with a blind curve a few yards away.

"One day you were thrilled with me for teaching you how to skate, and the next day you got mad because I wouldn't let you skate in the road."

Becca chuckled. "And several years later, when I was teaching my younger cousins how to skate, I wouldn't let them even get close to the road."

Ruth held her breath. "Do you recall the insight you shared with me later that day?" They had written down the words in Ruth's diary, and Becca had read them numerous times since—but not recently. Even if her daughter remembered the profound sentence, would she see the wisdom in it?

"I do." Becca carried the skates to the window and looked out at the driveway and the road beyond it. "When we're young, it's impossible to understand the dangers of everything that looks fun." Becca faced her mother and nodded. "I get it."

Ruth smiled.

"But I'm not giving up one ounce of *safe* fun."

Ruth laughed, tears brimming. "I fully agree. Not a single ounce."

Life Application

No matter where or how we live, temptation and sin find our children. The battle with a difficult teenager is never easy or fun, and we often need to look for more peaceful ways to get our points across. But the goal is worth the battle.

I remember arguing with my mom when I was a teen. Although I was furious with her at the time, some of the morals and principles I learned during those heated debates were deeply treasured later.

I once apologized to one of my adult sons, saying I wished I'd stayed calmer during his adolescent years. He laughed. "Mom, if you'd been any nicer to us kids, we would have run right over you and out the door toward trouble."

Parenting is a mixture of gentleness and warrior-like strength. None of us will get it right all the time. But our goal is to get as much of it right as we can, and to never give up trying—even when our children have kids of their own.

Ephesians 4:2 (ESV) says we are to do everything "with all humility and gentleness, with patience, bearing with one another in love." That applies especially to moms!

About the Author

Cindy Woodsmall is a *New York Times* and CBA best-selling author who has written seventeen works of fiction. Her connection with the Amish community has been widely featured in national media outlets. In 2013, the *Wall Street Journal* listed Cindy as one of the top three most popular authors of Amish fiction. Cindy and her husband reside near the foothills of the North Georgia Mountains.

9

The Invitation

by Julie Saffrin

"Plan on walleye for supper unless I catch one worthy of a taxidermist," Daniel told Elizabeth with a wink as he and their twenty-five-year-old son, Tyler, set off for Little Island.

Elizabeth never saw Tyler alive again.

She learned the sketchy details of her son's death from the water safety sheriff's report. A drunk driver had broadsided their boat, killing her only child.

Daniel had shown up at the funeral home brandishing a near-empty whiskey bottle, announcing to one and all that he was moving to Oregon. Alone. Elizabeth lost her son and her husband in one fell swoop.

Now, two years later, Elizabeth sat in her favorite chair, fingering a cream-colored envelope with the familiar handwriting of Tyler's former fiancée, Jenny. With trembling fingers, she opened the invitation.

Doris Thurston,
in honour of the late Dr. James Thurston,
invites you to the marriage of
her daughter, Jennifer Claire,
to
Commander Patrick Madigan, United States Navy
June the fourteenth
at five o'clock
Hotel del Coronado
Coronado, California

She still loved Jenny like a daughter, but wasn't two years too soon for her to be marrying someone else? Elizabeth had only parted with her mother-of-the-bridegroom dress last September.

A handwritten note slipped out of the tissue papers.

When Tyler and I were planning our special day, you told me that a wedding is the perfect time to surround yourself with those you love. You were, and are, an important part of my life. I miss you and would love to see you again. Please come.

Love,
Jenny

Elizabeth reread the invitation. *In honour of Dr. James Thurston.* Jenny had lost her father when she was a teenager. At twenty-two, she lost Tyler. Though Jenny would never be her daughter-in-law, Elizabeth was glad the young woman was willing to take another chance at happiness.

She looked up the airline's phone number and dialed.

The yellow taxi pulled up to the front of the century-old seaside hotel the morning of the wedding. Nicknamed "The Lady by the Sea," the Hotel del Coronado, with its glorious Victorian-styled architecture, seemed to welcome Elizabeth.

She entered the old-fashioned birdcage elevator. "I was a fool to have come," she said softly.

"Pardon me, ma'am?" the attendant said.

Elizabeth lowered her head.

"Let the late Lady carry your troubles away."

"I don't think that's possible, but thank you." When the shiny metal doors opened, she rolled her suitcase down the hallway.

She opened the door to her ocean side room. From the balcony she spied a wedding canopy on one of the sweeping grassy terraces. Her heart clenched.

After unpacking her bag, she walked down to the ocean that Magellan had named "peaceful" and let its calming waves wash over her. So much loss. Could she ever move on, as Jenny had?

That afternoon Elizabeth dressed in a navy suit and pearls. She arrived at the wedding a few minutes before five. With a six-piece stringed ensemble for accompaniment, an usher in dress whites seated her two rows from the front. On the bride's side.

The groom's party entered. Elizabeth was grateful dark-haired Patrick Madigan did not resemble her blond son.

Epaulets dangled from Patrick's shoulders. His white-gloved hand rested on his sheathed sword. Elizabeth inhaled. *It should be Tyler standing there. And I should be in the front row on the groom's side.*

The wedding march began and everyone stood. Elizabeth looked at Commander Madigan, waiting at the front. By the tears glistening in his eyes, it was obvious he loved Jennifer.

Elizabeth looked back at the bride and gripped the chair in front of her for support. Daniel, the man who'd abandoned her after their son's death, was walking Jenny down the aisle. Just like he'd planned to for Tyler's wedding.

At the altar, Daniel lifted Jenny's veil and kissed her cheek, then placed her arm in Patrick's. He walked over to Elizabeth, his expressive blue eyes filled with tears. She hesitated, tempted to make a scene the way he had at their son's funeral, then moved down a chair to make room for him.

She sniffed for the aroma of Daniel's best friend, Jack in a bottle, but the only fragrance was the salty air wafting off the ocean.

After a beautiful ceremony, the recessional began. Elizabeth ignored Daniel's outstretched hand, took the usher's arm, steered away from the wedding reception, and headed to the promenade deck that faced the sea.

Fingers touched her elbow. "Can we find some place to talk?" Daniel asked.

She spun on her heel and walked away.

He caught up to her. "Please, Elizabeth."

"What are you doing here?"

"I promised Jenny I'd walk her down the aisle."

She spewed a laugh as they reached the terrace.

"Let me explain."

"No." Elizabeth slammed her purse down on the ledge. "You lost the right to tell me anything when you left me in the middle of my grief."

"You're right." He leaned on the ledge and looked out over the water. "I was a coward and cruel. I'm so sorry."

She watched tumultuous waves pound the shore.

"But you had God to lean on, Liz." He picked at a tiny pebble in the concrete. "I didn't."

Elizabeth watched a naval ship inch across the horizon. Somewhere along the way she'd lost her faith in God. She'd stopped praying, reading the Bible, going to church. How could she lean on someone who'd failed to protect her from such deep loss and pain?

Daniel eyed her, then rubbed his fingers through his hair. "It was my fault."

Elizabeth squinted at him. "What are you talking about?"

"The accident. I caused it. I was so concerned about getting out of the way of the oncoming boat I didn't see the one behind me until it was too late." He drew his fingers across his wet cheek and sniffed. "That's why I left. I didn't want you to have to live with your son's killer."

"But the sheriff's report—"

"The sheriff wasn't there. I was." Tears dripped down his face into the corners of his mouth.

She looked away, feeling the warm wind against her face.

"We should have grieved together as husband and wife." Her fingers clung to the clasp of her purse as she moaned. "What have we got now? Is one dead child all that our history amounts to?"

He grasped her hand. "We were a couple before we had a son. I married you because I loved you. I still do."

"You made me hate you."

He lowered his head and sighed. "For a long time, that's what I hoped my leaving would accomplish." He inhaled deeply. "But Liz, I've changed." His shoulders straightened.

"Let me guess. You've become a Christian."

He nodded. "That's right."

She shook her head and folded her arms. Unbelievable. All the years she'd prayed for her husband's salvation, and they had to lose their son for her prayers to be answered.

He shoved his hands into his pockets. "When the boat got hit, I was knocked unconscious. I awoke feeling someone tossing me back into the boat. As I raised myself up I saw Tyler's hands slip from the port side. He used his last bit of energy to save me." Daniel hung his head. "Tyler gave up his life so I'd have another chance to find eternal life."

Elizabeth raised her hands to her face and sobbed. She felt Daniel's arms wrap around her. "Why did God take him?"

"I don't know. But I've learned that faith means trusting God with everything. Even losing our son."

He turned her toward the ocean, where the bright red sun touched the horizon. "Look out there, Liz. The Bible says the sea was made by the word of God. If we can't comprehend how the earth was created, how can we understand, this side of heaven, the reason for Tyler's death? Yet God tells us we can trust Him."

She leaned against him. Her entire married life she had prayed for this kind of union. Someone to confide her faith in, even her doubts. That man now stood next to her. She looked up at the cloudless sky. *God, how can I find my way back to You?*

"Tyler's life wasn't wasted." Daniel squeezed her shoulders. "Someday I'll join him in eternity."

She looked at the reception going on under the canopy. A verse from Song of Solomon came to her. *"He brought me to the banqueting house, and his banner over me was love."* Tears caught in her throat. She'd memorized chapter 2 verse 4 from her NKJV Bible after learning the song in Sunday school. Seeing the wedding banquet spread out before her reminded her that she'd been covered by God's banner of love … and that He wanted her to extend that love to others. Even to those she didn't feel very loving toward.

"I'm moving back to Tonka Beach in two weeks," Daniel said, "and opening a boys' fishing club on Little Island."

She looked up to him. "You're coming home to Minnesota?"

"If you're willing, I'd like to spend time with you." He nodded toward the reception. "If Jenny took another chance at happiness, don't you think we could too?"

"I don't know."

"I promise to never leave you again."

"I need time."

"I'll wait. Until you're ready, hold on to this." He placed

a small metal object in her palm. "Every time I look at it, it reminds me of how God can bring blessing out of sorrow."

"What is it?"

"The boat key."

She stared at it for a long time, her heart breaking.

Daniel stretched out his hand to her. "Can this be our moment of change, Liz?"

She returned his tentative smile and slowly entwined her fingers with his. Together they walked alongside the grand old Lady by the Sea.

Life Application

Sometimes all it takes to reconcile are a couple of words. But saying those words can be so hard.

Have you waited too long to apologize to someone, or are you angry with someone who has hurt you? Maybe it's your mom. Or your child. Or your spouse. Second Corinthians 5:18 says that God "reconciled us to himself through Christ and gave us the ministry of reconciliation." Jesus is the great Reconciler, the bridge between God and humans as well as in our relationships with one another. Because Jesus lives in us, we are called to a ministry of reconciliation.

Approaching someone you have wronged can be scary. Forgiving some who has hurt you deeply can seem impossible—it may not even feel right. But after prayer and repentance, you can be confident that Jesus has gone before you, laying the groundwork needed for reconciliation.

Roman arches are known for their durability because of the top center stone, called the capstone, that holds the two rounded halves of the arch together. Without the capstone, the arch sides would collapse. The same holds true for us. If we make Jesus the capstone in our relationships, He will draw us toward reconciliation with one another.

About the Author

Julie Saffrin is the author of numerous articles and short stories, including publications in *The Christian Reader, Chicken Soup for the Christian Woman's Soul, God Allows U-Turns,* and the *Minnesota Christian Chronicle.* Julie lives with her family in Minnesota. Visit her website at juliesaffrin.com.

10

Jesus and Bunny Slippers

by Lynette Sowell

The ringing phone jarred Sharon from sleep. Figuring her husband may be calling from his night-shift job, she scrambled to pick up. "Kevin?"

"No, it's Megan." Her thirteen-year-old stepdaughter's words were almost drowned out by blaring rock music in the background. "I need a ride."

Sharon shifted to look at the clock. Three a.m. "Let me talk to Jenna's mother."

"She's not here. Please just come and get me."

"All right."

"I'll be waiting outside." *Click.*

Sharon stepped into her slippers and padded down the hallway. "Sure, kid," she muttered. "Just hang up. No 'thank you' or 'I appreciate your help.'" She paused when the baby inside her moved. "I know it's late, sweetheart," she said, rubbing her abdomen. "Or early."

After grabbing her purse from the kitchen counter, Sharon headed into the dark and rainy night. She stepped carefully over the muddy driveway, trying not to slip.

Something had to be wrong for Megan to swallow her pride and beg Sharon to pick her up. She'd talked of nothing but Jenna's sleepover for the past week.

Patches of light from the streetlamps served as guiding beacons as she climbed into the car. Life with Megan hadn't been easy. Sharon never seemed to please the girl. She hadn't been prepared for her stepdaughter's outbursts, stomping down the hall, or mealtimes when Kevin tried to pry conversation out of them both.

I need Your guidance, Lord, in doing my part to make us into a family. If she heard *You're not my mother* one more time, she was positive she'd scream. She started the engine and pulled onto the wet street.

Rain streamed down the windshield and tears streaked down Sharon's cheeks. At least the three of them attended church together. But Megan always joined up with her youth-group friends the moment they arrived, leaving Sharon to wonder what tales the girl would tell about her "wicked step-mother."

A whisper echoed in Sharon's heart. *Even if you might never be a mother to Megan, be Jesus to her.*

Sharon cringed.

She turned the car into the entrance of the upper-crust housing development. She'd driven past it many times, trying not to covet the grand homes she glimpsed over the tops of the privacy fence. No way could she and Kevin afford a place in this neighborhood. Especially not with Megan's recent demands for high-priced clothing and fashion accessories. She'd been jockeying her way up the social hierarchy in school, the latest effort being tonight's exclusive sleepover at Jenna's.

Sharon pulled up to the curb in front of a two-story house ablaze with lights. Five cars crammed the driveway, and another one rested partially on the lawn as if a giant's finger had pushed it out of the way.

A backlit figure leaned against a wrought-iron lamppost in the yard. Sharon unlocked the passenger door, and the figure trudged across the lawn and climbed into the car.

Megan's hair lay like spaghetti strands on her shoulders. Smeared mascara rimmed her brown eyes. She bit her lower lip as she slammed the car door. The scent of cigarette smoke clung to her like an invisible cloud.

Sharon's first urge was to ask who'd given her the garish makeup, who'd been smoking, and where in the world was Jenna's mom? Instead she gritted her teeth and made a U-turn.

"You're mad." Megan's chin jutted out in defiance.

Sharon took a deep breath. "I'm tired. And worried." The rhythmic swish of the wiper blades filled the silence.

"Oh, c'mon, don't tell me you're not going to freak out."

"You needed to come home, so you called. You did the right thing."

"I didn't do it for your approval."

Sharon sighed. *How can I be Jesus to this obstinate girl?*

She reminded herself of Bible stories in which Jesus loved the outcast, the unlovable, the angry. He saw their true needs, not just what could use changing on the outside.

Sharon wanted to grab a moist towelette from her purse and give it to Megan so she could clean up her face, but stopped herself. What was Megan's true need?

A police car, lights flashing, zoomed past them on the rain-slick street.

"I wonder where they're headed," Sharon mumbled.

Megan felt her stepmother's eyes boring into her through the darkness. Sharon wasn't so bad when she wasn't trying to force the three of them to act like one big happy family. Megan didn't buy the loving stepmom routine.

When her dad and Sharon got religious and starting dragging her to church, she found the youth meetings interesting. Megan even prayed a little on her own. But she *had* to belong in Jenna's crowd. Sharon had no clue what it felt like not to belong anywhere.

"The cops are probably headed to Jenna's." Megan hated the little-girl sound to her voice. "The party was fun at first. But then some kids showed up with pot." Megan wanted the bucket seat to swallow her up. "Jenna doesn't do stuff like that. Not that I know of anyway."

Why wasn't Sharon saying anything? Megan braced for a lecture. Instead, her stepmom said, "I could use a bite to eat. You hungry?"

Megan tried not to let her jaw drop open. "Yeah."

They turned into the parking lot of an all-night diner, the old-fashioned kind like she'd seen in the movies Granddad watched.

Megan flipped down the visor and looked at her reflection in the mirror. "I can't go in there like this. I look like a drowned raccoon."

Sharon pulled a small packet from her purse. "Here."

Megan took the towelette and wiped off her smudged makeup. Three hours ago she'd felt glamorous. Now she looked like a six-year-old caught playing with her mother's cosmetics.

Inside the diner, they slid onto red vinyl seats in a corner booth. Condensation dripped down the windows as the air conditioner fought off the humidity. Under the table Megan saw Sharon's pink bunny slippers, their floppy ears covered with mud.

Dad had given Sharon those slippers on Easter morning. She'd squealed and hugged them after she pulled them out of the gift bag, and she wore them all the time at home. Sharon went bonkers when Megan had accidentally let a drop of ketchup splash onto one. Now the pair of bunnies looked like they'd frolicked in Mr. MacGregor's garden. If something like that happened to Megan's favorite shoes, she'd probably cry for a week.

Megan eyed the menu and hoped Sharon wouldn't mind if she ordered a double burger and cheese fries. Dad and Sharon always talked about money. They worried about it a lot. After the baby came, money would be even tighter.

"Order whatever you like." Sharon scanned the menu. "I think I'll have mozzarella sticks and a chocolate shake."

"Ooh." Megan let herself grin. "You're living wild tonight."

Sharon curled a wisp of honey-colored hair around one ear and smiled.

"I'm sorry," Megan blurted.

"For what?"

"For making you come out tonight and ruining your cute slippers." Megan's face grew hot.

Sharon glanced at her feet. "No problem," she said, though her smile had disappeared. "I can run them through the washer when we get home."

Lord, she's opening up a little. For the first time in ages, she's concerned about someone else's feelings. What now? Sharon tossed questions around in her mind while Megan ordered.

She'd almost wanted to cry when she saw the slippers in the glow of the diner's parking lot lights. Running them through the washing machine would probably destroy them. But tonight went beyond caring about material things.

Megan made little shapes out of the straw wrapper. "Are you gonna tell Dad about the party?"

"Of course."

"I'll be grounded."

"Maybe. He and I will talk about it first."

Their food arrived, giving them a welcome intermission. Sharon took a sip of chocolate shake and groaned.

"Brain freeze?" Megan nibbled on a cheese fry.

"Yes." Sharon grinned. "But it's chocolate, so I don't care."

Megan frowned. "We didn't pray over the food." She returned a fry to her plate.

"You're right." Sharon bowed her head.

Before she could begin, Megan prayed, "Lord, thanks for this food, and for Sharon coming to get me. Amen."

Sharon opened her eyes and looked across the table. Tears streamed down the young girl's cheeks. "What's wrong?"

She rubbed her forehead as though massaging a headache. "I don't always know what I'm doing."

Sharon reached for Megan's hand and squeezed. To her surprise the teenager didn't pull away. "I don't know what I'm doing sometimes either. I just know that I want to live my life to please Jesus. And I want to see other people the way He does." She inhaled deeply, weariness catching up with her. "I'm still learning. Someday I hope you'll see a difference in me." Fresh tears pricked her eyelids.

"I don't hate you."

"I know." Sharon released Megan's hand and took another sip of her milkshake. One step at a time, she reminded herself.

While they ate, they talked about nothing in particular. The trip home was spent in the kind of silence that comes with unspoken understanding.

Sharon felt the baby move as she hefted herself from the driver's seat. The rain had let up, but puddles still remained in the driveway. She slogged her way to the sidewalk.

"You okay?" Megan looked back from the front porch, where she stood on the top step.

"The baby's just reminding me it's bedtime." She unlocked the front door and wondered if the evening's timid tap dance of communication had been worth it.

Sharon kicked off her muddy slippers, then followed her stepdaughter to the kitchen.

Megan leaned on the counter. "Hey, Shar '?"

"Yes?"

"Can . . . can I feel the baby move?"

"Sure." She laid her hand over Megan's and pressed it to her abdomen.

The girl's eyes rounded. "Oh, wow," she whispered.

"I think that's a heel." More movement. Time slowed to a crawl in the little kitchen. Sharon met Megan's awestruck gaze. "Amazing, huh?"

"Yeah." She pulled back her hand. "Hey, thanks for stopping for food on the way home. It was kind of fun doing something without Dad. Just us."

Megan surprised Sharon with a hug, then pattered to her bedroom.

A week later, Sharon found a present on the kitchen table. Her name was written on an envelope propped up against the paper-covered lump.

"It's not my birthday," she said as she opened the card.

Dear Sharon,

Thanks for coming to get me the other night. In spite of what you think, I've been listening in youth group. It's hard when your friends want you to act one way, and you know Jesus wants you to act another. Don't be too tough on yourself. I do see Jesus in you.

Hugs,
Megan

Inside the floral wrapping paper was a new pair of bunny slippers.

Life Application

Blended families are common in our society. How can we best respond to the jumbled emotions that result from school and sports and carting kids back and forth to visitation? Even a well-adjusted child may react sometimes.

Like Sharon, stepparents don't always know what to say or do. You walk a tightrope. You don't want to suffocate your stepchildren and try to be their "new best friend," but you don't want to be distant and seem uncaring either.

What should you do when your children by love and marriage show an ugly attitude or cast hurtful words in your direction? What if the atmosphere is as tense as a piano wire, or even just filled with awkward unfamiliarity?

"Be kind and compassionate to one another, forgiving each other, just as in Christ God forgave you" (Ephesians 4:32). Even to the people who live with us? Especially to them. Though you may not be a biological parent, you have assumed the role of a parent at your spouse's side.

"Be completely humble and gentle; be patient, bearing

with one another in love" (Ephesians 4:2). Be willing to admit you don't have all the answers, and let your fallibility show.

Not only do you belong to your immediate family—your spouse and his or her children—you also belong to the family of God. A little forgiveness and mercy go a long way. After all, God accepted you into His family through His limitless forgiveness and mercy. Couldn't you do the same and show your stepchildren acceptance?

"If it is possible, as far as it depends on you, live at peace with everyone" (Romans 12:18). Choose your battles. Sometimes, no matter how carefully you respond to a situation, you're not going to make the children happy. Ask the Lord for guidance, to see if you're doing your part to promote peace. Avoiding confrontation doesn't mean happiness reigns. But carefully searching your heart and weighing your motives for confronting a stepchild will help contribute to a peaceful home.

As you seek to become more like Christ, He will enable you to live as an example before your stepchildren. They'll see Jesus in you.

About the Author

Lynette Sowell is an award-winning novelist who lives in central Texas with her own blended family: her wonderful husband, a son and a daughter whom she calls her "kids by love and marriage," and five zany felines. You can learn about her writing at lynettesowell.com.

11

Reaching for Redemption

by Lori Freeland

*L*iz sat in her car, staring at the pristine white Lexus parked in front of Tally's Tea and Treats. She'd run in for a mini Mother's Day cake to surprise Grams—the only mother she had left—and had three more errands she needed to finish on her day off.

But something about the country-club blonde next to the Lexus snagged her attention and now she couldn't look away. Even if all she could see was the woman's back.

Hair cut in a sleek bob, and dressed in white linen slacks and a mint sleeveless blouse, the blonde could've been a carbon copy of the upscale shopping plaza's usual customers. Except for her shoes. The red-and-silver stilettos belonged in a night club, not on this middle-aged woman's feet.

Those shoes left a knot in Liz's gut.

The woman leaned into the car, then walked to the front and fumbled to prop the heavy hood in place. Tucking a chunk of salon-perfect hair behind her ear, she peered at the engine, giving Liz a glimpse of her face.

That knot turned to lead. "No." Liz swallowed hard and squeezed the steering wheel. Her mother couldn't be here. Her mother lived in Italy.

After slamming the hood, the woman pulled a phone from her pocket, made a call, and faced Liz's direction.

No denying it now. The prodigal mother had returned. On Mother's Day weekend no less.

Phantom pancakes lodged in Liz's throat, throwing her back to the worst morning of her life. It didn't matter that her last breakfast with her mother happened ten years ago. Liz remembered every word. Every smell. Every kick of her heart against her ribs.

"I need to leave," her mom had said. "I did my time. You're all grown up, Lizzy. You don't need me. You're seventeen." Then she'd cut her plate of pancakes into neat little squares, like her words hadn't just wrecked Liz's world.

"God," Liz whispered, pulling herself back to the parking lot. "Why are You doing this to me now?" How many times had she begged Him to bring her mother back? How many times had He left her disappointed?

Sweat dampened her neck. Her fingers tingled. The barely-there breeze blowing in her car window couldn't compete with the stifling Texas spring heat or the feeling that she was folding in on herself. She cranked the engine and flipped the air on high.

But she didn't leave.

Her mom … No, not her mom. She lost the right to that title the morning she walked out. *Tracy* sagged against the Lexus and wiped her forehead. A few shoppers stopped, probably to offer help, but Tracy held up her phone and shook her head.

Why didn't she go into the tearoom? Or any other store? And why was she wearing those ridiculous shoes?

Because she always wore ridiculous shoes. That was one of the good memories Liz had of her childhood.

"Back out of the parking lot," Liz told herself. The out-of-commission Lexus was not her problem. "She forgot about you. Forget about her."

The car stayed in park. Her foot stayed on the floor mat. "You did fine without her. You didn't need her at seventeen. You don't need her at twenty-seven."

So why couldn't she leave?

Over by the Lexus, Tracy looked up. Her gaze bounced across the parking lot. And hit on Liz.

Liz's chest exploded. She pressed a hand over her heart, as if she could stop the way it raced.

Tracy took a step forward, then paused, her face a mix of fear and hope.

With a groan, Liz turned off her engine, got out of the car, and kicked the door shut with her plain-Jane sandal. Needles of pain shot through her toes. She stomped across the space to the Lexus.

"Lizzy. Baby." Tracy gave her a tentative smile and reached out.

"Why are you here?" Liz gripped her keys.

Tracy dropped her arms and her smile.

This woman, who used to be her mom, didn't look much older than when she'd left. Other than a line or two next to her eyes, they could've been sisters. It had always been like that.

"You … you're all grown up." Tracy stumbled over her words.

Acid filled Liz's stomach and she pushed it into her tone. "I asked why you were here."

"Grandma gave me your address." Tracy leaned closer. "I was coming to see you."

Liz took a step back and pointed her keys at Tracy. "You don't talk to Grams. And she knows I don't want to talk to you."

Shifting in those dance-club heels, Tracy wiped her sweaty forehead. "Can we go somewhere cooler?"

"Sure," Liz said. "You go in the tearoom. I'll go home."

"I apologized to my mother. I'd like to apologize to you."

The acid in Liz's stomach turned molten. "It's too late."

"Please," Tracy said. "Can we talk? For a minute?"

"I don't have anything to say. Not anymore." It had taken her years to stop yelling at her mom in her head.

"Triple A can't get here for an hour. I have something to say to you. Could you listen?"

"You didn't listen when I asked you to stay." Liz turned and walked away. Could her feet be any heavier? Her shoulders any tighter?

"You're right." Tracy called after her. "I don't deserve your time. But I'm asking you anyway."

The desperate tone in Tracy's voice halted Liz's sluggish steps and she turned around. "Fine. Then you'll leave and we'll pretend you never came."

"If that's what you want." Tracy pocketed her phone, locked her car, and headed into the diner two stores down from Tally's—where Pancake Fest was running all week.

How sick. And ironic. *God, why?* Liz trudged behind Tracy. *Why now?*

A wearied waitress led them to a quiet booth in the corner. "The pancake breakfast is on special all day and—"

"Iced tea, please." Liz put her hand up. She'd choke on the pancakes. Or vomit them all over Tracy. Although there was some appeal to that.

Tracy ordered iced coffee and waited until the waitress left before she asked, "You don't eat pancakes anymore? They were your favorite."

Liz leaned back in the booth and crossed her arms. "I stopped eating pancakes the morning you left."

Tracy glanced away. "You know, I was eighteen when I had you. Hadn't even graduated. I had to do everything alone."

"You probably shouldn't have gotten in the backseat of Don's car then." Liz curled her toes in her flat sandals. No ridiculous flashy shoes for her. No backseats either. Or boyfriends.

The waitress returned with their drinks.

Liz added sugar to her tea, then crossed and uncrossed her legs. "I'm waiting for your great excuse."

Tracy took three packets of Sweet'N Low and opened

each one slowly, like she was buying time. "I know you think I'm a terrible person. A bad mother."

"If you're waiting for me to disagree, the place closes at nine." Liz took a sip, and the sweet tea burned going down her throat.

Tracy pushed her glass to the side and wiped her hands on a napkin. "I thought I'd given up my life for you and I wanted it back."

"I figured out all on my own that you were sick of me. But thanks for sharing." Liz scooted to the edge of the booth.

"Walking out on you was stupid and selfish." Tracy stood and blocked her way. "You were more important. But I didn't understand that."

Liz tensed.

"Please. Hear me out. Then you can leave."

Liz sat, but at the edge of the booth, her feet pointed toward the exit, her mind already in the car.

"I don't want to be that person anymore." Tracy folded and refolded her napkin. "I'm sorry I can't take the last ten years back." A tear rolled down her face. "It wasn't right, what I did. You were my daughter. You *are* my daughter. I can't change our past, but I'm willing to work for our future."

All the nights Liz had sobbed in bed imagining a moment like this, making herself sick wishing for it, churned the tea in her gut. "Do you really expect me to instantly let go of how you made me feel?"

"No. I don't expect that at all." Tracy blotted her face with the wrinkled napkin. "But I miss you. And I'm so sorry."

Her mother's expression of repentance didn't bring the relief Liz expected. It just made her ache all over again. "I can't do this."

"You already did." Tracy wrapped her hand around her glass. "I apologized. You listened."

"So what now? You pop back in once in a while for a meet-and-greet with your grandchildren?" If there ever were any grandchildren.

"I'm staying," Tracy said. "I start a new job Monday."

"You're moving back?" Those phantom pancakes made an encore in Liz's throat.

"Maybe one day you can forgive me."

The hope in Tracy's eyes cut Liz like glass. She stared at the pattern etched into the opaque partition separating their booth from the next. This was what she'd wanted, right? Her mom back. "I don't—"

"I just want a chance to prove I'm sorry."

Liz swallowed. "I may never be able to forgive you."

"That's okay. Maybe we can start over. As adults. Have lunch sometimes. Catch up. Talk."

"Talk?"

Tracy nodded. "When you feel like it."

"I don't feel like it now." Liz slid out of the booth.

"Lizzy?" Tracy held out a piece of paper with a local phone number scrawled across it. "Call me. Anytime. I'll wait."

Taking the paper, Liz shoved it into her pocket. "Maybe. That's all I can give you right now."

"It's more than enough." Tracy's smile was less tentative this time.

Liz rushed out of the diner and slid into her car.

You wanted your mom back. God's voice brushed over her soul. *Give her a chance.*

"Seeing her hurts." She brushed away the tears on her cheeks. "A lot."

Trust Me, not her. I'll protect you.

Liz pulled out the paper. Her fingers shook, but she managed to punch the numbers into her cell.

"Hello?" Tracy answered on the first ring.

"Next week." Liz fought to keep her voice steady. "I'll meet you next week."

Life Application

Tracy returned to seek forgiveness from Liz and make amends. God is the king of second chances. We all make mistakes. We mess up in our relationships and in our decisions. First John 1:9 says, "If we confess our sins, he is faithful and just to forgive us" (ESV).

While Liz wanted her mom back, pain and fear kept her from embracing her mother's return. Tracy had broken her trust. God is the author of trust. When we can't trust people, we can always trust Him. His Word promises, "The Lord … will never leave you nor forsake you" (Deuteronomy 31:8).

Cling to the one constant in your life and keep your heart open to forgive.

About the Author

Lori Freeland is a writing teacher and coach for the North Texas Christian Writers and a contributor to Crosswalk.com and Believe.com. She's addicted to flavored coffee and imaginary people. When she's not writing inspirational articles, she's working on several young-adult novels. Visit her website, lafreeland.com, or look for L. A. Freeland on Facebook.

12

You Can Take this Job and Love It!

by Martha Bolton

*N*ext!"

Melanie stepped up to the counter at the employment office, clutching a classified ads page.

"How can I help you?" the clerk asked.

"I-I'm Melanie Baker," she said, hoping the stutter didn't make her sound as unprepared as she felt. "I'd like to apply for one of the jobs you have advertised."

"I hope it's not the administrative assistant position. I just gave that to the fella in front of you."

"No, that isn't it."

"EKG technician? We have several of those jobs available."

"No, not that either."

"The zoo is looking for someone to clean the elephant cages. Don't suppose that was it, huh?"

Melanie shook her head, her nose crinkling at the thought. "It was for the position of Mother."

The clerk chuckled. "Well, cleaning cages and picking up a teenager's room—not a lot of difference." She plucked a typed sheet of paper from a rack on the wall. "So, what kind of experience do you have?"

Melanie gulped. "Um … I taught preschool once."

"Perfect! That'll qualify you for both positions. Sure you don't want to reconsider the zoo job?"

Melanie shook her head. Ever since she was a little girl, she had dreamed of becoming a mother one day. That's why she got so excited when she saw the ad. She didn't know if she had what it took, but she needed to give it a shot.

"Okay," the clerk said, looking over the job specifications. "It says here the applicant for the position of Mother should be an experienced cook."

"I used to work the day shift at an all-night diner."

"Only the day shift? Hmmm. I don't know. A mother's kitchen is a twenty-four-hour operation, all three shifts, three hundred and sixty-five days a year … three hundred sixty-six on leap years. You up for that?"

Melanie hesitated. "I'd get *some* time off, right?"

The clerk broke out in hysterical laughter. Melanie hadn't meant for the question to be funny.

"How are your listening skills?"

"I have perfect hearing."

"Are you planning to keep it?"

"Of course."

"Well, that might disqualify you, given the possibility of garage bands, slumber parties, youth groups, video games. I guess we could waive that requirement if you got yourself a pair of industrial-strength earplugs."

Melanie nodded. "I'd be willing to do that."

"Good. Now, how are your fashion skills?"

Finally something Melanie was skilled at. "I don't mean to brag, but I have a degree in fashion design."

"Really?" The clerk raised an eyebrow. "Well, you should throw it away. It'll only depress you when your teenager insists on picking out his own clothes."

Melanie sighed.

"Now, is a spotless home important to you?"

"I do like to know where everything is at all times."

"So do kids. They like to know that their socks are in the living room, their shoes are in the hall, and their schoolbooks are in the microwave."

"A place for everything and everything in its place, huh?" Melanie wondered if this job might be a little more work than she'd figured on.

"What about counseling skills?" The clerk leaned her elbows on the counter. "Have you ever helped someone get through a nearly impossible situation—like, say, algebra?"

"Actually, I flunked algebra. Will that go against me?"

"Depends. How are you at math word problems?"

"Not my strong suit … but there are tutors for that, right?"

The clerk scoffed. "If you can afford them. You got a millionaire husband by any chance?"

Melanie shook her head.

"Some other high-paying job then?"

Melanie clenched her clammy hands together. "I was hoping I wouldn't have to work outside the home. I'd like to be available for the children."

"Well, whether you get another job or not, you'll have to be around anytime the family needs you. And not everyone's ready to deal with all the whining that comes with that two a.m. earache, the six a.m. stomachache, and the eleven p.m. toothache. And that's just when Dad's sick. When the kids get sick, it's even busier!"

"When does a mother get to sleep?"

"Oh, she can get a full eight hours—on that night when the last child moves out and before the next morning when the first one moves back in."

Melanie took a deep breath. What was she getting herself into here? "If a mother does all that work, the pay must be terrific!"

The clerk laughed so hard she held her side. "Did you say … pay?"

"She does get paid, doesn't she?"

"Of course! She gets to keep all the change she finds in the washing machine."

"That's it?"

"Hey, on a good day she can spin-dry three or four bucks easy."

"How about vacations? She gets some of those, right?"

"In the summer, a mother can spend days planning, packing, and preparing, then sleep on hard ground in a tent or in a cheap, tiny, noisy motel. And then unpack and do mounds of laundry afterward. Oh, and on the way there and back, you'll hear 'Are we there yet?' about a million times."

Melanie gasped. "What do I do then?"

"Oh, that's easy. Just say, 'Yes. Get out.'" The clerk grinned.

Melanie bit her lip. "Doesn't the job offer *any* days off?"

"You get one. Mother's Day. Provided you cook your meals the night before."

"Sick days?" Melanie asked in a weak voice.

"Oh, mothers have lots of days when they're sick."

She grit her teeth. "I mean, if she's sick, she gets the day off. Right?"

"Sorry, no. She still has to work."

Good grief! How could a person be expected to work in such ridiculous conditions? Had the labor union heard about this? "If the job requires all that, why would anyone in their right mind want to do it?"

"Oh, I haven't told you about the benefit package yet." The clerk beamed.

"No benefit package could be worth all that!" Melanie stood and turned to leave.

Just then, a man entered the office. A young girl with a bobbing blonde ponytail stood beside him. "Mommy! Mommy!" She ran behind the counter and jumped into the clerk's arms.

"Hello, sweetheart." She squeezed the little girl tight, then smiled at Melanie over her daughter's shoulder. "These kinds of benefits."

Melanie's heart swelled. "Where do I sign up?"[1]

Life Application

Motherhood may be one of the most rewarding, challenging, admired, underappreciated, overloaded, difficult, and fun job a woman can have. The Bible tells us the children of the Proverbs 31 woman will "arise and call her blessed" (verse 28). A lot of mothers would be happy if their children would just *arise!*

If you've been blessed to be a mother, you probably already know how special that job is. If you're a mother figure in someone's life, you know it too. It's not an easy job. But everything worthwhile requires hard work, dedication, and prayer. And maybe some help.

You wouldn't be here if it weren't for the woman who raised you, and you wouldn't be the person you are today without her influence. If possible, show her your appreciation in some kind of tangible way. If you can't demonstrate your love to your own mom, do something special for someone else's mom. Or reward yourself for investing in the life of a child.

As demanding as it can be, motherhood is a job to be cherished and honored. So take this job … and *love it!*

---

1 This short story is based on a comedy sketch written by Martha Bolton, originally published in The *"How'd I Get to Be in Charge of the Program"* *Help Book*, (Lillenas Publishing Company, 1988).

About the Author

Martha Bolton is an Emmy-nominated and Dove-nominated former staff writer for Bob Hope and the author of eighty-eight books of humor and inspiration. Her novel *Josiah for President* was published by Harper-Collins/Zondervan in 2012. She is writing her second novel, *The Home Game*, which will open as a musical in 2016. Martha was the writer for *The Confession Musical* script based on Beverly Lewis' best-selling trilogy. She also wrote the script for *Half-Stitched, the Musical,* based on Wanda Brunstetter's book *The Half-Stitched Amish Quilting Club.*

13

Lightning

by Mary DeMuth

The day Daddy died, Mama called me Lightning. Libby'd been my name till that day, the day that transformed our happy Midwest life into charred smoke.

Daddy worked the fields from black dawn to black dusk. I don't think he ever saw the sun angle through the windows of our white clapboard home, never did see the dust particles frolic at the sun's touch. Only the moonshine glimmered by the time he came in for supper, and by then the dust had settled, as if frolicking had tired it clear out.

One night the sky threatened rain—a thing most farmers welcomed. Daddy wanted his fields to be ready to drink in the showers, wanted to plant one last row before the first spat of water hit his hat.

He and Mama, they had a deal. He tilled the soil; she paid the bills. Time to time, they'd have a money feud—right at the field's edge, where the gravel driveway kissed loamy earth. I'd hear 'em clear from the house carrying on about Daddy wanting more farm implements and Mama saying, "No, not this year."

She'd come back tear stained and toil over the bills on the wide-planked table in the kitchen. Daddy'd return to the field and till.

I don't know why my father stayed out that rainy night, why he kept sowing row after row of seed corn. Perhaps hard labor became part of their unspoken pact, the tilling and toiling rhythm that marked their easygoing animosity. Maybe it was a simpler notion—that whenever he held a yellow corn seed, even under roiling clouds, he felt compelled to work until his fingers numbed. Problem was, that night his fingers did numb.

Maybe he possessed that mad spirit most farmers have, that if something needs doing, it must be done to the very end of a man's tenacity.

I've calmed my tears by believing Daddy dirtied his fingernails for all of us kids. His sacrifice, his soil-stained face, his narrowed eyes from too much sun squinting … all these cobbled together was his gift to us. Harrowing and sowing and uprooting and burning—all for our hungry mouths, our bare-naked feet, our gangly limbs that kept on growing.

I heard the thunder first. I crashed out of my room and stood at Mama's side, shaking like an oak leaf in a windstorm.

"This too shall pass, Libby. God's just rearranging His furniture is all." Mama petted my tangled head as if her absentminded touch would settle my nerves. But my knees kept at their quaking and my skin crawled with fear.

Didn't she know thunderstorms meant God was angry? I

couldn't bear a furious deity. With every growl of thunder, I felt sure I had done something to rile Him up.

That night, God must have been relocating a lumbering sideboard because of my coarse words with Jeb, my younger brother. I knew I shouldn't have called him a stinky rat fink when he won Monopoly fair and square.

My father would still be alive if I could've just held back my flapping tongue, sure as pie.

Daddy must've seen the lightning, must've watched it flash across the sky in rickracked abandon. Head forward, rain pouring from his hat brim, he planted beautifully tilled rows of corn-to-be, precisely one foot apart, seemingly unaffected by the mayhem above him.

Mama paced the living room in front of the big picture window, stopping now and again to say, "Mercy!" Why she held up her hand as she gazed on inky fields, I'm not sure. There was no sun to shield her eyes from, only distant flashes of lightning. Like a movie flickering on the faces of upturned showgoers, Mama's face was illuminated on and off, on and off. God took her flash picture about a hundred times. And every time lightning lit her, worry etched itself further into the contours of her weathered face.

I was standing beside her when we saw a bolt fly straight from God's fingertips, pointing catty-corner this way and that. When Daddy looked up, illuminated by the light rushing toward him, Mama gasped. It was as if the Lord was telling him planting time was over. God's jagged finger of light pointed right at Daddy's hat and knocked him dead.

Just like that.

Mama and I raced out there. In my father's hand were a scatter of corn seeds, charred, smelling like burnt popcorn. I don't know why I remember the smell more than Daddy's contorted face. Call it a child's view of life, I guess. He lay stiff and flat at the cornfield's farthest edge. One burnt seed had fallen into the last row, as if Daddy couldn't stand leaving his sowing job undone.

His final act on this earth had been to plant a seed.

We kids dug a seven-by-three-foot hole right in the middle of the cornfield. Daddy's dirt-brown coffin was buried in the muddied earth. We figured he'd want to be sown that way.

I sniffed in my sorrow, trying to be brave, but the tears came fast.

"I declare, Lightning, you're a fine kettle of fish, boo-hoo-ing like that."

Did Mama just call me Lightning?

"C'mon, Lightning, it's time to do chores," she said as plain as dirt.

I didn't correct her. You just don't reprimand a grieving mama. But every day after, she hollered that name when I was in the fields to bring me back into the kitchen to cook. She even called me Lightning in town, in front of everybody. The name stuck to me like tar.

When Mama named me Lightning, I somehow took on its properties. I became caustic, unpredictable, destructive.

That summer, the corn shot up greener than ever. A windstorm with fistfuls of hail leveled the field right before harvest, leaving Daddy's graveside stark against the Midwest sky, surrounded by penitent corn plants.

Except for one.

The charred seed planted by my daddy just before he got electrified stood tall and proud, in rigid defiance of the storm, its leaves waving like arms at the Almighty.

We managed as best we could, but life was a struggle. Mama got a job at the cannery and tried hard not to get her arm chewed up in the machinery, like Elmer Singleton. She moved us all to town and sublet our land, something my brother Jeb held against her forever and a year.

Despite my efforts otherwise, I grew up, tall and lilting like a willow tree, and I caught the eye of Sage Williams. "Lightning," he said, hat in hands, "I'd be most privileged to call you my wife. What d'ya say?"

"Yes" is all I said, as I brushed away a tear.

We moved into the clapboard house, my childhood home, bordering the fallow cornfield. Four children later—Sunny, Windy, Autumn, and Edlef (don't blame me for that one; it was his granddaddy's name)—the thunder of God's wrath started boiling around our home. But only Sage and I heard its rumble. My nagging, his yelling, my swearing, and his slamming all boiled together in the cauldron of our marriage.

Must've been my name that got us into this, I figured. That fire in me that first caught Sage's interest recoiled, changed courses, burned his ego, and singed his tenderness until he became just like me: a lightning rod of angry words.

Outside, where the gravel met the dust, we argued the same feud Mama and Daddy had—toiling and tilling.

"The bills are piling up," I hissed.

"I'm doing the best I can," he yelled. "What do you expect?"

"It's not good enough."

"Maybe I'm not good enough. Maybe you'd be happier if I was gone."

The children didn't hear the tired escalation; at least that's what we thought, until Edlef came toe to toe with us there under God's blue canopy. He rubbed his eyes and stuttered, "Our lives are stormy, sure enough. You and Daddy are like lightning and thunder. I can't abide it."

As Edlef's tears dripped down his ten-year-old cheeks and hit the warm, thirsty earth, I knew one thing. I hadn't called Sage a stinky rat fink, but I might as well have. Guilt shot through me, pinning me to the gravel.

Lightning had taken Daddy from me, not God. God wasn't angry. I was.

And now, lightning was threatening to take another father from his family. I could not bear my children suffering the scouring loss of their daddy, not if I could help it.

I excused myself from Sage and Edlef and walked to the center of the barren cornfield. I dirtied my knees at Daddy's graveside, begging the God of lightning to spare our family, to save our marriage. I stood, hands on hips, still feeling despair course through my veins. I sighed, then shouted to the heavens, "I'll do anything to make things right. Anything!"

In my heart, I seemed to hear God say, *This is holy ground, Lightning.*

I shook off my shoes in hesitant reverence. The dust around Daddy's grave gritted my toes. "I don't want anger to be my fallback anymore. Forgive me. And teach me another way. Please. Not for my sake, but for my family's."

I felt clean after saying those words, way down deep inside, like God had scrubbed my heart with a Brillo pad full of baking soda. I still ached. But the darkness had lifted.

I'd gone into the barren cornfield to do business with the Almighty as fiery Lightning Williams. Barefooted, I walked the dusty path back to the clapboard house as just plain Libby.

Life Application

Anger, if left unchecked and unconfessed, can lead to disaster, particularly when it's attached to the tongue. Scripture tells us in James 3:6, "The tongue is a flame of fire. It is a whole world of wickedness, corrupting your entire body. It can set your whole life on fire, for it is set on fire by hell itself" (NLT). When we give in to our anger and then explode on our loved ones, we risk alienating and possibly losing key relationships.

As mothers, we tend to set the tone for the environment of our families. The old saying "If Mama ain't happy, ain't nobody happy" rings true. Our primary job, then, is to tend to our hearts for the sake of our family's harmony.

So how can we positively deal with the anger that lurks inside us?

We can confess it to a trusted friend, asking her to keep us accountable when we're tempted to explode. We can practice the discipline of silence, realizing that not every angry thought needs to be spoken. Proverbs 17:28 reminds us, "Even a fool who keeps silent is considered wise; when he closes his lips, he is deemed intelligent" (ESV). We can write out our anger in a notebook, letting it dissipate on the page. Storytellers can write an angry scene, playing out our anger instead of letting it take over our lives. Or we can be like Libby and holler our anger at God, asking Him to bring about lasting, sweet change.

Those who were raised by angry parents have a natural tendency to treat their own families the same way. But the truth is, you don't have to live angry. There is hope when we come to the Lord, fall on our knees before Him, and let Him fill us with His love.

About the Author

Mary DeMuth is a veteran blogger and the author of thirty books, both nonfiction and fiction. She has spoken around the world about how to live an uncaged, freedom-infused life. She makes her home in Texas with her family. Find out more at MaryDeMuth.com.

14

My Son, the Swamp Creature

by Pasquale "Pat" Russo

*J*essica stood in the upstairs hallway, staring at the towels covering the bathroom floor. "Michael has struck again," she muttered under her breath.

Turning toward her bedroom for a laundry basket, she shook her head over the same questions that had haunted her ever since her adult son returned home.

What force compelled him to consistently use a dozen towels for one shower? What caused a scholarship recipient to go through a handful of washcloths shaving his head? And what had transformed her cum laude graduate with a master's in theater into a clueless zombie that never hung up his wet towels?

If Warner Brothers were filming an animated feature about Jessica's morning, steam would be coming out of her ears.

As she dumped the contents of the basket onto her bed, her cell phone vibrated. "No one should talk to me right now," she told the phone.

As she headed back to the bathroom with the empty basket, she noticed a trail of wet footprints leading from the bathroom to Michael's bedroom.

She knelt on the bathroom floor with an exasperated sigh and flung the still-damp towels into the basket.

Mixed in with the everyday towels she found two of the soft, thick burgundy ones she loved to sink her face in, all of the cream-colored embroidered washcloths reserved for company, several large beach towels, and even a Christmas tea towel.

As she lifted the heavy load, Jessica caught a whiff of musty washcloths. While awkwardly juggling the large basket, she bumped into the doorframe and it slipped from her grasp.

A slew of reactions passed quickly through her head—from kicking the basket down the stairs to dumping the entire mess onto her son's bed. Instead she walked back to her bedroom, grabbed her phone, and composed a text message to Michael.

Pile of eight towels & ten cloths on bath floor. Again. Fine: $2 each = $36. Put payment on kitchen table by morning. I AM NOT THE MAID!

Rereading the message, Jessica debated upping the fine to five dollars. Deciding to save that for next time, she hit send. She dragged the basket into Michael's bedroom and closed the door. Then she grabbed her sweater, stuffed the phone in her purse, and stormed out to her car.

Jessica snuck into her friend's living room, found an empty chair, and caught the last minutes of the ladies' Bible study. Sharon shot her a quick smile from a few seats away. When the group broke for coffee, Jessica checked her phone. Seeing two messages and a missed call from Michael, she shoved the phone back into her purse.

"Where were you?" Sharon asked as she handed her a cup of coffee. "You're never late for Bible study."

"Rough morning." Jessica took a sip. "What'd I miss?"

"We watched a great video about the Prodigal Son. It focused on the attitudes and motivations of each of the characters. I'd never heard about anyone but the father and the son before."

"Did it mention the Prodigal Son's mother? The one ready to evict him after he'd been back home for a few weeks?"

"Uh-oh. What happened?"

"Michael's a swamp creature. He turns the bathroom into primordial ooze every day. We may start spawning mosquitoes soon. I'm about to call the store that Wile E. Coyote uses and get a towel rigged with explosives that goes off when he drops it. Maybe then he'd get the point."

Sharon laughed. "I love your sense of your humor! But if that's the biggest problem you're having with Michael living at home, it's a small price."

"I suppose. But I've mentioned the towel problem to him several times."

"Maybe you should switch to decaf," Sharon said as she took her cup back. "Come on, Jess. He's not doing drugs. He's not out partying every night. He doesn't ask for money. He's working three jobs while auditioning for movie roles and waiting for his big break. A lot of mothers would trade you in a heartbeat."

"Really? Who? I'd take Anna's daughter. In fact, I'll take both of her girls. They'd never leave the bathroom looking like a biohazard."

Sharon touched her arm. "No, they'd drive you into bankruptcy on cosmetics and clothes!"

"Do you think they'd let me use their nail polish? I'd be okay with bankruptcy if I could look stylish."

Sharon put a hand on her hip. "We both know it's not the towels in the bathroom irking you. What's got you all worked up?"

Hearing her phone buzz, Jessica looked at her watch. "I gotta go. It's my mom's birthday, and I'm taking her to lunch."

"What restaurant are you going to?"

"Whichever one she picks."

Jessica pulled away from the assisted-living center and into traffic. "There might be a wait at the restaurant," she said, glancing at her mom. "It's a popular spot. Are you sure that's where you want to have lunch?"

"I can't think of anything better than having my grandson bring my lunch to the table," Mom replied, checking her face in the passenger-side mirror.

"I don't know whether he's working today."

"I do. He called me on his way there to wish me a happy birthday."

Jessica felt an ache in her heart. She said nothing for the remainder of the brief drive, but her memory plunged her into recollections of the sweet spirit that characterized Michael as a youngster.

After parking in front of the restaurant, she got the walker out of the trunk and gave her keys to the valet. Once inside, she looked for a place for her mother to sit for the ten-minute wait for a table.

"Mom! Grandma!" Michael called out. "No wait for you today. You get our special VIP birthday seating."

Taking his grandmother by the arm, he gently led her to a table and eased her into a chair. As he planted kisses on both of her cheeks, she giggled. "I'll get you some water."

He rushed off, but reappeared quickly. After delivering the beverages, Michael expertly described the day's lunch specials and made suggestions from the menu that fit his grandmother's diet.

When he went back to the kitchen with their orders, Mom reached across the table and squeezed Jessica's hand. "You have such a special boy. And you've been a wonderful mom. I couldn't ask for a better birthday present than being with the two of you."

Jessica smiled and ducked her head, her cheeks burning with embarrassment.

Dear diary, she thought. *Today I received a compliment from my mom.*

Had her compliments to her son become just as rare?

After delivering their meals, Michael sat with them, talking about his jobs and a few recent auditions. His grandmother—once active in community theater—asked him questions about the roles and the producers. They all laughed at some of her audition stories.

They skipped dessert, opting for coffee. Still, Michael brought his grandmother a tiny slice of strawberry cheesecake with a candle in it and softly sang "Happy Birthday" in her ear.

When Jessica opened the folder containing the check, there was a note instead of a bill.

I'm SO SORRY about the mess, Mom. Don't mean to be such a slob. I will do better, I promise. Thanks for your patience. I appreciate being at home … even if it doesn't show.
    Love,
    Michael
    P.S. Keep the change.

Under the note were two crisp twenty-dollar bills.

Life Application

Having an adult child living at home can be challenging. First Peter 2:17 offers a solution: "Show proper respect to everyone."

Ephesians 6:4 encourages parents not to scold or nag their children, but to bring them up in loving discipline, which helps avoid making them angry or resentful. Ephesians 6:1–3 tells all children—including adult children—to honor and obey their parents.

What negative attitudes might be keeping you from living at peace with your children? Regardless of their ages or where they live, they need your encouragement … and your respect. What can you do to change the atmosphere in your home and make it a place your family members love to be?

About the Author

Pasquale "Pat" Russo is a veteran writer who has held editorial leadership roles at Fortune 500 firms. His debut novel, *Another Vanishing Act,* is a humorous look at how one man's trouble plays out in a senior living community amid a mature cast of oddballs. Find him online at http://pasquale-russo.com.

15

The Gift

by Christina Weeks

I cover Noah with a blanket, careful not to touch him. He looks like a content five-year-old, cozy in his bed. Dinosaur pajamas. Freckled nose. Brown eyes outlined by thick lashes. But I've learned in our six months together—his quiet countenance masks a wounded soldier.

"You're sure you're not too hot?" I ask.

He stares at me, then gives a slight head shake.

"If you need anything, Dad and I are down the hall. Okay?"

He blinks—his way of saying yes. My fingers itch to tousle his bangs, but I let my arms rest at my sides.

Blake joins us. "Here's your bedtime snack, buddy." He sets a paper bag on the table next to Noah's bed.

We wait like puppies hoping for a treat. Will we get an acknowledgment? Something that tells us Noah knows that he's safe? And that he believes there's enough food?

He continues the blank stare. Like a warrior home from a tour of duty, his thoughts are still on the battlefield.

"I'll leave the hall light on and the door cracked," I say. "Remember—Mom and Dad love you. You're in your forever home."

Noah doesn't try to get out of bed or ask for a drink of water. I'd be thrilled if he did.

"Sweet dreams." I turn off the light, then shuffle to the living room. Blake places his hand on my back. I slide under his arm and rest my head on his shoulder. At least we're in this together.

When I return to Noah's room the next morning, cellophane wrappers circle his empty snack bag. Cracker crumbs dot the floor. I peer under his bed. He's hidden what he didn't eat in between a couple of stuffed animals and a dump truck.

Who could blame him? Hoarding's natural when you've been starved.

Noah breathes a heavy snore. Blankets are pushed toward the end of the bed, and one foot hangs over the side. He's peaceful, eyes closed, mouth open. I don't want to wake him. We've learned the hard way that mornings are rough.

But I can't avoid it forever.

"Noah, honey," I whisper. "It's time to wake up for school."

His eyes fly open, pupils darting left and right. He scrambles to the corner of his bed and shoves a pillow barrier in front of his pajama-covered legs. His hands shield his lap.

My throat clenches. "It's Mommy. Are you ready to get dressed?"

Recognition spreads across his face slowly, like butter melting. His shoulders relax a little. He rubs his eyes with his fists, then moves to the side of his mattress. He sits on the edge like a withered old man—all of his energy sucked away.

"I picked out clothes for you. They're on the chair. Shorts and a T-shirt."

He leans forward and rests his chin in his palms. I step toward him, my arms ready to hug him into healthiness. But last time I touched him, he screamed and bit and scratched.

"I'll be in the kitchen when you're ready."

As I leave his room, the counselor's advice rings in my ears. *Give him time. Watch for his clues. Discover his triggers. And pray.*

I've cried out to God countless times, kneeling on the frontlines with Noah, encountering enemy fire, wondering what to do. My precious Lord always gives me words to say, actions to take, insights to understand. Sometimes at the eleventh hour, but He's proven faithful every time.

And God loves Noah. Even more than we do. He is working hard to reach him, to show His love, to comfort him. I see it in the mini breakthroughs we've had.

Lord, help me remember what You've done for Noah. And for me.

Even with so much evidence of God in Noah's life, there are times when I wonder, *Am I what he needs? God's love is sufficient. But is my love enough? Am I up to the task?*

Blake's in the kitchen with coffee made. He hands me a cup. "How'd this morning go?"

I shrug, trying not to let the weight of unmet hope crush the joy of our small wins. "Same as yesterday."

"I'm sorry." He steps close, sweeps hair back from my shoulder, and rubs my neck. "You're a natural mother."

A smile overcomes my frown. "Thanks. I needed that."

"You're doing great." He kisses me on the cheek. "And speaking of motherhood, what do you want to do on Sunday?"

"Sunday?"

"It's your first Mother's Day."

I've been too distracted to even notice. "I don't know." Pulling from his embrace, I lean against the counter. "Noah hasn't fully bonded with us yet. I don't want to confuse him. Or make him feel awkward." I stir cream in my coffee, the spoon clanking against the ceramic mug. "Maybe we should wait 'til next year."

Noah appears in the doorframe, a ghost of silence. He doesn't have on the outfit I picked out for him. He never does, so I'm not sure why I expected today to be different. As always, he wears the long-sleeved tan shirt and blue jeans he's worn every day since we brought him into our home.

Blake crouches beside him. "Hey there, buddy. How ya doing?"

The question is rhetorical, of course.

He's still locked in his cage. How do I show him he's free?

I raise my eyebrows, trying to not let my disappointment show. "Ready for breakfast?"

He shakes his head.

"Not hungry?"

Another headshake.

"Okay. Well, here's your backpack with your homework. There's a bologna-and-cheese sandwich and fruit snacks. Let's head to the car, all right?"

Noah stays in his spot.

An alarm ticks in my head. When he's not in survival gear, Noah gives us robot-like obedience.

"Sweetie?" I ask. "Do you need something?"

He stares.

I kneel in front of him. "Are you okay, Noah?"

His chin drops. He's holding something behind his back. Staring at his feet, he brings forward an orange construction paper cut-out. It's creased in squares as if it has been folded in his pocket. He hands it to me.

Though Blake is nearby, the room shrinks to just me and Noah. I reach for his gift. "For me? Did you make it at school?"

His gaze is still to the floor, so I can't tell if he blinks. I take the paper from his hand.

Hapy Mothr's Dy runs off the page. The *H* is large at the top, the *y* squished in the bottom corner. Two stick figures stand underneath. A boy in a tan shirt and a woman with brown curlicue hair. Arrows point to both. One says *Noah*. The other says *Noah's mom*.

Tears blur the images, and my heart thumps. "Thank you, Noah," I whisper. "I love it. I'll keep it forever."

Blake kneels next to me and places a hand on my shoulder. His grasp is warm and reassuring.

Thank You, Lord.

Noah raises his chin and smiles.

A second gift! But more than that. A miracle. A sign. We're going to be all right.

Noah's mom.

Best gift ever.

Life Application

At what point do you become someone's mother? For many, it's hearing the first cry in the delivery room. For others, it's during the adoption entrustment ceremony when a newborn is placed in your arms by a loving birth mother. For some, the journey to being called mom is a little longer.

No matter how you earn the title, motherhood requires faith, trust, strength, and endurance. Whether waking multiple times to feed a crying baby, struggling with a toddler's tantrums, or soothing deep wounds of an older child, motherhood stretches us beyond our comfort zone and often leads us to ask, *Am I enough?*

The answer is a resounding yes.

Hebrews 13:20–21 encourages us, "May the God of peace … equip you with everything good for doing his will, and may he work in us what is pleasing to him, through Jesus Christ, to whom be glory for ever and ever. Amen."

Each of us has been hand picked by the Father to serve as

our child's mother. Whether born naturally to us or brought to us through adoption, our children have been given to us by the Lord. And when we seek His guidance, He equips us to be the best mothers we can be.

So take courage. You are enough.

About the Author

Christina Weeks is author of CoffeeCupFiction.com: "stories the length of your mug." She's also published in short fiction and commercial publications. In addition to being a writer and full-time mother, Christina has worked at Walt Disney World, flown in a stunt plane, and raced a stock car. Follow Christina at Facebook.com/CoffeeCupFiction or Twitter.com /ChristinaWeeks1.

16

Pieces and Quiet

by Barbara Curtis

Cookie pieces. LEGO pieces. Piano pieces. In the midst of them all, Kate Porter was falling to pieces.

Was it too late to huddle in a corner and weep over what she'd gotten herself into? With Matthew in the middle of the floor, encircled by a trail of LEGO bricks and toy cars, Kate couldn't even get to a corner without injury. And even if she did manage to crawl over there, it wouldn't be quiet. Not with Tara banging through her daily piano practice. She'd never be able to sneak off alone anyway, as Kellianne hung on to her everywhere she went. Why didn't her life with a good husband, three kids, a dog, and even the white picket fence mirror the all-American dream portrayed in books and movies?

She loved her family. But at the moment she would also love a piece of sanity.

Footsteps thudded onto the front porch. Kate grabbed her wailing toddler and flung the door open before her husband grasped the knob. "Paul, I'm so glad you're home!" She handed him the child wrapped around her waist. "Here." She loosened the little girl's hands clinging to her neck and reached for Paul's briefcase. "Trade you."

He released his grip on the handle and swapped briefcase for squalling girl. Then he stretched around Kellianne to give Kate a kiss. "Is dinner almost ready? I only have about an hour before I have to go back to the office. A guy they're hoping to hire flew in for a second interview and he's only available tonight."

Kate closed her eyes and drew in a long, slow breath. So much for a walk around the block. Alone.

"Kate?"

She opened her eyes. "I'll have dinner on the table by the time you finish saying hello to the kids and get washed up."

"Can you take her back?" He handed off Kellianne, who had quieted in his arms.

"Sure."

"Hey, Daddy!" Tara called from the living room. "Listen to my song. It's going to be for my recital."

Recital? Were all those hideous chords and key changes actually meant to be a song? Tara plunked out her notes again, and Kate wanted to cover her ears. Whatever happened to sweet, lyrical melodies?

Within minutes Kate had dinner on the table and Paul and all three kids were seated. During the blessing, the room was quiet, except for Paul's calming voice offering thanks to God. Kate squirmed in her chair. She was grateful for what she had. Really she was.

As soon as the kids echoed Paul's amen, they were back to their usual mealtime noise. Chattering. Spilling. Complaining. And Kate's seemingly endless reminders of proper etiquette.

"Slow down and chew your food, Matthew."

"Tara, don't talk until after you've swallowed the food in your mouth."

"Kellianne, you eat your peas. The dog has her own food."

As soon as dinner was over and the kids excused, they went back to their predinner noise. Clashing chords on the piano. Toy cars zooming and crashing across the living room floor. And screeching from Kellianne as she stepped in front of the zipping vehicles.

Kate couldn't take another minute of this chaos. How was she going to get through the entire evening without exploding?

"Sweetheart, before you head back to work, do you think I could take a short walk around the block?" In response to Paul's startled look, she added, "Please?"

"Of course." He winked. "Just don't forget to come back."

"Thanks." Kate gave him a quick kiss, grabbed her keys and phone, and stuffed them into her pockets.

"Where's Mommy going?" Kellianne whined behind her. "I want to go!"

"No, sweetie," Paul said as Kate scurried down the front steps. "Mommy's going by herself this time."

Halfway up the block Kate could still hear crying and repetitious chords emitting through their open living room window.

She looked back at their little house with the white picket fence. She appraised the rest of the fairy-tale setting as well—the dented minivan in the driveway, the bicycle with a flat tire abandoned on the lawn …

Maybe if she'd looked closer at the fine print, she would've known constant noise was included in the all-American dream. Or that by the end of the day she'd look like the flowers Paul had given her last week did now—wilted and tired.

She glanced at her watch and walked faster. Within fifteen minutes she'd have to be back.

A body jumped out in front of her from behind a bush. She screeched.

"Hey, Mom!" her son yelled.

"Matthew Lincoln Strong, you scared me half to death!"

"Great! That was my plan."

She sighed. Her oldest was nine already. When had he gotten up to her shoulders?

"Where are you going?"

"Just for a short walk around the block—to enjoy the quiet."

"I like quiet too. My teacher says I'm the quietest kid in class."

Kate sent him a questioning look.

"It's true."

They walked down the street, Matthew chattering on endlessly. She actually enjoyed it. When did she ever have uninterrupted time to simply listen to his heart?

"Mom!" Running feet came down the sidewalk and caught

up with them. "I'm glad I found you." Tara panted. "I just *had* to tell you about my piano lessons. Mrs. Bailey won't be there next week, so I'm practicing twice as hard this week. Daddy said I could tell you if I didn't bother you." She gave Kate a sweet smile, exposing a missing tooth. "I'm not bothering you, am I?"

"Of course not. Would you like to walk with us?"

"Yeah!"

Kate took Tara's hand, so small and soft. Perhaps the hand of a future accomplished pianist. Tara swung Kate's hand high in the air, then swung it back down.

"Did you know I wrote that song?"

"All by yourself?"

"Yep. I have words too."

"You do?"

"But you can't hear them yet. They're for you at the recital."

"You wrote a song for me?"

"Uh-huh. It's called 'I'm Thankful.'"

"And what are you thankful for?"

Tara giggled. "You always tell us to be thankful to Jesus for what we have. And I'm thankful that you're my mom."

Kate stopped midstride and pulled her daughter into a big hug, her heart nearly bursting. Her little girl was living out the lesson she had taught. One apparently Kate herself hadn't mastered.

Oh, Lord, forgive me for a heart of ingratitude. I do thank You, so much, for what You've given me.

"There's Mommy," Kellianne shouted from Paul's back as he trotted toward them. "Faster, Daddy, faster!"

Kate lifted a brow as he caught up to them with his squirming passenger.

He gave her a sheepish look. "I know you wanted to be alone. But Kellianne wouldn't stop crying. She missed you." He stuck a large sunflower under her nose. "I did too."

"We picked it for you, Mommy," Kellianne announced.

Kate glanced at her watch, then at Paul.

He took her hand. "It's okay. We have time." He squeezed her fingers. "And even if I am late, I wouldn't miss our walk for anything."

"I'm glad." She'd only had about two minutes by herself. But Kate wanted this time together to last. This was much better than any peace and quiet she would have had by herself.

She had all she needed right here. Her family. And God's peace.

Life Application

Have you ever had a day like Kate's, where all you dreamed of was just a few minutes of peace and quiet, some time to be alone, away from life's demands? Even though you love the people God has placed in your life, it can be quite a challenge balancing responsibilities with times of refreshment. How can a mom—or anyone, for that matter—find peace in the midst of chaos?

God's Word gives us the answer.

"Above all these things put on love, which is the bond of perfection. And let the peace of God rule in your hearts, to which also you were called in one body; and be thankful" (Colossians 3:14–15 NKJV).

Love, peace, and thankfulness are intertwined in these verses. All three fit perfectly together for the life God wants us to live.

When you have a rough day and don't know how you'll make it through, remember to put on love, to let God's peace rule in your heart, and to be thankful.

See what a difference it makes.

About the Author

Barbara Curtis lives in Connecticut with her family. She loves editing and writing, especially fiction. This devotional gives her a chance to fulfill Psalm 34:3: "Oh, magnify the Lord with me, and let us exalt His name together" (NKJV). She has additional stories published in *21 Days of Grace* and *21 Days of Christmas,* the first two books in the Fiction Lover's Devotional series.

17

Where I Belong

by Jan Cline

Carlson. It was just a dot on the map. One of a hundred or more that covered Kaylie's computer screen. She pressed a white sheet of paper against it and used the tip of her pencil to trace a line from her home, along all the little dots, to Carlson, on the other side of Nebraska.

If only it were that simple to travel there. It seemed so close when tracing the journey on paper. But the map program's calculation said it was 568 miles from the place she was to the place she very much wanted to be.

"Kaylie, breakfast is ready," her mother called from the bottom of the stairs, just as she did every morning. The smell of French toast and scrambled eggs floated up the stairs.

"Coming," Kaylie shouted back as she slipped on her jean jacket. She zipped shut the small suitcase on her bed and hoisted it to the hardwood floor. One last look before leaving. Everything was neat and tidy. It wouldn't do to return to a messy bedroom. And she didn't want her mother to have to clean up while she was gone—although it might make her feel better to fuss over it a bit.

Kaylie pulled the comforter back and mussed the sheets. Then she pulled a sweater and shirt from her drawers and tossed them on the floor and chair. She scattered papers and pens across the top of her desk. There. Mother would enjoy fixing everything, even if she grumbled about it.

She carried her suitcase downstairs, parked it by the front door, then hurried to the kitchen. The food on the table incited growls and rumbles from Kaylie's stomach. This would be her last chance for a while to eat anything she wanted, and she planned to have all the syrup-laden French toast she could swallow.

Mother's forehead wrinkled. "Are you ready for this?"

"Yeah." She downed a few gulps of freshly squeezed orange juice.

"I wish *I* was."

Kaylie rolled her eyes. "Can we please not talk about it right now?"

"If your father were here—"

"Well, he's not. But if he was, he would have approved of this decision. I know it." Seeing the pained look in Mom's eyes, Kaylie softened her tone. "I'm eighteen now. I can make my own choices." She had to stand her ground about this, even if there were tiny doubts bouncing in her mind.

Mother finished unloading the dishwasher as Kaylie ate the last few bites of her eggs. After patting her full stomach, she took her dishes to the sink and wrapped her arm around her mother's waist. "Let's go."

Mom sighed. This would be a long day for her, but necessary. And in Kaylie's mind, divinely appointed.

The hours crept by. With each passing mile in the car, Kaylie's anticipation at seeing Jenny inched closer to becoming anxiety. Would this reunion be all she hoped? It didn't matter. This was the only chance she had to build a bridge with Jenny, regardless of the risks. No turning back now.

After counting a hundred power poles on the roadside, Kaylie broke the silence. "Are you all right?"

Mom shrugged. "Sure. I'm just nervous for you. And for me too, I guess."

Kaylie twisted in her seat to study her mother's expression. "Why?"

Mom scrunched her face and let out a slow breath. "I'm nervous I'll lose you." A tear escaped her eye.

Kaylie straightened her posture. "But they said the surgery wouldn't be dangerous for me."

Mom wiped away the tear and gripped the steering wheel. "That's not what I'm worried about. You've been through sickness and broken limbs before. I always placed you in God's care and knew He would keep you safe."

"Then what's the problem?" The minute she asked the question, the answer came to her. Since the day they found Jenny, or rather she found them, her mother had been on edge. Kaylie hadn't put the puzzle pieces together until this moment. Her mom was afraid she would have to give up her place in Kaylie's life and let Jenny take over.

Mom cleared her throat. "I know it's not unusual for children who find their birth parents to want to be with them instead of their adoptive parents. If that happens to you—"

Kaylie held up her hand. "Wait a minute. You don't think I'll choose Jenny over you for a mother, do you?"

Mom bit her lower lip, confirming the outrageous thought.

"No way is that going to happen. I don't care how many kidneys I give her, you are always going to be my mother."

Tears flowed down Mom's cheeks. "If you don't stop making me cry, I'll have to pull over."

Kaylie laughed, feeling the emotional crisis was over. They drove the last hour in silence. Kaylie dozed, not waking until the car came to a stop.

"We're here." Her mother spoke as if they had arrived at someone's funeral.

"Well, I guess this is it." Kaylie mentally prepared herself for a long day of tests and pokes and prods. "Thanks for driving me here." She smiled at her mom, then bounced out of the car before things could get uncomfortable again.

After Kaylie got checked in, examined, and briefed, the time came to meet Jenny for the third time in her life. In a few hours, their lives would be intertwined like never before. As the nurse wheeled Kaylie to the small room on Ward 5, her heart beat hard against her chest.

Mom followed and waited outside the door.

Jenny lay still in her bed, pale and yellow skinned. She looked up when Kaylie entered. "Hello."

"Hi."

"It's not too late to back out." Jenny's voice was strained and weak.

Kaylie looked away and stared out the window. "I know." It was all she could say. Her heart would break if she spoke another word.

She took a seat in the corner. Tension filled the room like a cold fog. After a while, Jenny drifted off to sleep. Kaylie watched her breathe. This was the woman who gave birth to her. She wished she'd known her before this situation brought them together.

Mom came up beside her. "Kaylie? It's time for you to go to your room now. The nurse said I could take you."

She looked up at her mother. "Jenny said I don't have to do this."

"She's right. It's not too late to change your mind. She needs you. But you have to do whatever you feel is right for you."

Kaylie hung her head. This could be her only opportunity to be more to her birth mother than a memory. She wasn't about to miss out on that.

Mom crouched down and looked into her eyes. "Are you positive you want to do this?"

"Yes. I am."

As Mom tucked her sheets in around her, Kaylie stared out the window of her hospital room into the dark night. She swallowed back the tears so her mother wouldn't see how scared she was.

"Good night, honey. I'll be here bright and early to see you into surgery." She kissed her forehead. "I love you."

"I love you too, Mom." Kaylie watched her walk out the door. She knew her mother loved her. If Jenny loved her too, this would be a lot easier.

God, I thought it was Your will for me to save Jenny's life. So why am I having doubts now?

A golden light filtered in the window, reflecting the setting sun in the mirror above the sink. Kaylie thought back to the first time she met her birth mother, just a few months ago.

Jenny had seemed indifferent about whether Kaylie offered her kidney or not. Jenny's sister, Barbara, had offered to donate hers instead. But Kaylie had convinced everyone to do it her way. Jenny never even thanked her.

Sleep came quickly after the nurse made her swallow a small pink pill. Kaylie dreamed about walking along a river with her mom. While they fed the ducks, as they had dozens of times before, she told her mother, "Jenny gave birth to me. But you've given me life."

She fought to wake up from her thick sleep. Sun streamed in the window, making it hard to open her eyes all the way.

Mom stood by her bed, her face somber. "It's all right to go back to sleep. The surgery has been … postponed." She stroked Kaylie's forehead.

"What?" She tried to sit up, but Mom guided her back down.

"I'll tell you about it later. You need your rest."

Kaylie managed to raise her head off the pillow. "Tell me now. What's happened? Is Jenny—"

Mom fiddled with the blanket. "She's fine. She just changed her mind. She doesn't want your kidney. Her sister's going to do the surgery instead."

"Why?"

Mom stroked Kaylie's hair. "Honey, she … she said she … she doesn't want to see you again."

The room spun and Kaylie rubbed her temples to make it stop. "I don't understand."

Mom leaned down. "I'm so sorry you had to go through this." Her eyes welled with tears.

How could her birth mother do this? It was as if Jenny were giving her up all over again.

Mom must have sensed her thoughts. "I'm here for you, sweetie. I will never reject you."

Kaylie recalled the dream and remembered the words she'd said to her mother. It was true. Mom had given her the life she was destined for. Her real mother—the one God had designed for her to have—would always be there for her. Her eighteen-year-long sacrifice was God's gift.

The ride home wasn't silent this time. They talked of many things they'd never shared before. Their time together would be better than ever. Kaylie would make sure of it. It would be her gift to the one who gave her life.

Life Application

Have you ever wished you could choose a different family? There's nothing quite like knowing you are in the family God designed for you. We don't always appreciate the legacy our parents provide. Moms offer love and guidance, and if they fear God, they point us in the path of righteousness.

We can choose to accept the inheritance of God's blessings from those who give us physical or practical life, or we can go our own way and risk losing all that has been generously gifted to us. Whether it is birthed or bought, our heritage is locked into the women our hearts call Mom.

God has fashioned an inheritance just for you. His inheritance is eternal. His gift to us, through our choice to be part of His family, is to live with Him for eternity. We will be lavished with His presence and be forever glorified with Him in our heavenly home.

Our decision to accept God as our Father, and embrace the sacrifice of Jesus, makes our heritage a binding legacy. No matter how much provision we receive from our earthly parents, the family life to come will be beyond our dreams.

About the Author

Jan Cline is an author and speaker from the northwest US. She has numerous articles, short stories, and devotionals to her writing credits, including two devotional books. She is currently working on two historical novels. Jan speaks to women's groups, writers' groups, and conferences. Visit her at jancline.net.

18

Treasures

by Larry J. Leech II

Faye put down the pen and massaged her wrist. "I'm done," she said to the assisted-living worker sitting on the edge of the bed.

"Are you okay?"

"That was a lot harder than I thought."

"Most people don't bother." Wanda patted Faye's hand. "I'm proud of you."

"Thanks. I like to have my affairs in order."

Organizing her room here at Happy Hearts was one thing, but dividing her worldly possessions was another. Since the birth of her first child, Faye had put a lot of thought and prayer into what treasures she would store up for Amber. Two years later, when Faye gave birth to another girl, she adjusted her list. Then a surprise. A boy. Someone for Joe to pass along his possessions to.

"Are you ready for them to come in?"

"Help me into the chair first." A stack of a hundred index cards in her hand, Faye eased out of the bed. She shuffled, with Wanda's help, to her wingback chair by the window and collapsed into the well-worn cushions. "Give me a minute."

"Whenever you're ready."

"Will you fan out those chairs in front of me for the children?"

For years, Faye had prayed about this moment. She spent hours deciding which of her children would receive each item she'd accumulated during her life. Furniture. Scrapbooks. Pictures. A few personal possessions. Family heirlooms. A little bit of money.

Most of the decisions were easy. Her sewing stuff would go to Amber, a stay-at-home mom married to a surgeon. Elizabeth, the free spirit who loved to travel, would receive her crafting supplies. Her husband's tools and fishing gear were earmarked for Thomas, of course—the struggling creative who did things his way.

Other decisions needed more time in prayer. Elizabeth and Thomas had repeatedly argued over who would get the antique curio cabinet.

Amber and Elizabeth both wanted the four-poster bed that had been in the family for more than seven decades. They had slept in it during their preteen years. Before Amber used it the first time, Faye copied Proverbs 3:24 from her Bible onto a sheet of flowery stationery and taped it to the headboard: "When you lie down, you will not be afraid; when you lie down, your sleep will be sweet." The girls told Faye numerous times over the years that they prayed that Scripture every night.

All three of the children wanted the grandfather clock. When each one reached age thirteen, Faye sat with the birthday child in front of the clock and discussed the importance of time. At the end of the talk, she gave them an engraved plaque with Ephesians 5:15–17 from the English Standard Version: "Look carefully then how you walk, not as unwise but as wise, making the best use of the time, because the days are evil. Therefore do not be foolish, but understand what the will of the Lord is."

She'd always planned to give her eldest child her most prized possession. But two days ago, she received a different answer in a dream. She prayed about it for a full day. Then yesterday, in a conversation with a friend over lunch, she felt as if God confirmed the dream. She hoped the "losers" wouldn't get mad.

Faye loved all of her children. And she thoroughly enjoyed visiting with each one individually, along with their spouses and kids. But group visits usually ended up with so much sibling animosity she couldn't wait to get back home. She hoped the warring would stop after she was gone. And that today wouldn't end with one or more of her children storming out.

"Let them in," Faye said quietly.

After Wanda left, Faye ran her fingers along the edge of a silver picture frame on the table next to her chair. A faded photo of Joe rested inside. She touched his smiling face. "I'll see you soon, my love."

The door eased open and Amber's head appeared. "You ready for us, Mom?"

Faye nodded. Her three children entered the room.

"Please, sit." Faye pointed to the metal chairs.

When she shivered, Amber grabbed the quilt at the end of her bed and placed it around Faye's shoulders before taking her seat.

"Thank you all for coming today. With your busy schedules, it's tough to get the four of us together in the same room." She pressed a hand to her chest to suppress a cough.

Thomas straightened the collar on his polo shirt. "Why are we here?"

"To go over these." Faye held up the index cards.

Amber smoothed her skirt. "I can't believe, after all these years, we finally get to see what's on those cards."

Thomas glanced out the window. "I don't know why you couldn't have just mailed them to us."

"Because I wanted my children together one last time."

Amber leaned close. "Are you sure you want to do this right now?"

Faye looked at her older daughter's beautiful face. "I don't have much time left."

"Don't be silly." Elizabeth interlocked her fingers in her lap. "You're gonna make it to one hundred, like you've said you would ever since I was a little girl."

"I wish that were true." Faye thumbed the edge of the top card. "I'm just grateful for the chance to do this before I go."

She shuffled the cards, wanting the distribution to be random—or, rather, in God's divinely chosen order. She resisted the urge to put the card with the grandfather clock on the bottom.

Lord, help me get through this.

She flipped over the first card. Her set of china. With a half smile, she handed the card to Amber. She barely glanced at it.

The next card was for Thomas. When she handed it to him, he let out a big whoop and pumped his fist.

"What'd you get?" Elizabeth asked.

"Dad's lathe."

"Good. I wouldn't know what to do with a lathe."

Thomas patted his sister on the leg. "You'd give it to me."

Faye flipped over the next card. The grandfather clock. So soon? She gulped, then handed the card to her son.

He stared at it, stone faced.

Amber leaned over his shoulder. "You got the clock?"

Thomas grinned.

"I can't believe you're not dancing around the room," Elizabeth said.

"Well, since you mentioned it …" He stood.

"Sit down," Faye said. "There will be no gloating over who gets what."

Thomas took his seat.

For the next hour, Faye passed out the rest of the cards.

When she handed Amber the last one, Faye slouched in

the chair, thankful she'd finished and the kids didn't fight. All she owned now were a few clothes, a couple of blankets, and the pictures here in her room.

She pointed at the cards each child held. "I'm sorry you had to wait so long to get those."

Amber touched her knee. "I'd rather have you than all of these things put together." She glanced at Thomas's stack of cards. "Including the clock."

Faye laid a hand on her daughter's. "You're so sweet. But even if I could live forever, I'd pass." Her voice faltered. "I miss your father terribly."

Thomas stood.

Amber looked up. "Where are you going?"

"I need to stretch my legs. These chairs are uncomfortable."

"Before you go, I want a picture." Faye struggled to stand. "My camera's in the top drawer of my dresser. Let me get it."

Thomas put a hand on her shoulder. "We can use our cell phones, Mom."

"Oh yes, I forgot."

"You sit right there," Amber said. "We'll gather around you and I'll set the timer."

Thomas helped Faye into her chair and kneeled to her right. Elizabeth crouched to her left. Amber set her phone on the dresser, hit a button, and said, "Ten seconds. Everyone smile."

When Amber slid into place, Faye grinned. "My last treasure."

"And we'll all get our own copy."

Life Application

While many parents store up earthly riches for their children, Scripture encourages us to store up riches in heaven (Matthew 6:19–21). No one can fault a mother for wanting to divide the family heirlooms among her children. After all, we can't take material things to heaven. But do you have spiritual stories connected with your earthly possessions?

Have you considered distributing your things before you pass and using that time for one last teachable moment with your children?

About the Author

Larry J. Leech II is a ghostwriter and writing coach who started his career more than thirty years ago. After twenty-three years of working as a journalist for daily newspapers and an international magazine, he moved into full-time book writing and editing. He also teaches frequently at writers' conferences around the country.

19

A Good Mom

by Roxanne Anderson

Christine tried to focus on driving in spite of the tears that distorted her view of the road. She wiped them away roughly, gripped the steering wheel more tightly, and guided her battered Toyota carefully off the overpass to merge with the heavy morning traffic headed into the city.

It felt so wrong, leaving her two kids in day care to go to work. Even after a whole month, her new routine seemed anything but normal. Unfortunately, she had no choice. She'd finally made the painful decision to file for divorce, and she had to live with the consequences.

This was never what she wanted, she thought for the millionth time as she glanced over her shoulder, bullied her way into the far left lane, and accelerated. She wanted to be the stay-at-home-mom in the kitchen baking bread, the wife with the candlelit dinner on the table at six when her husband came through the door. She wanted to homeschool her kids, and for her and Steve to be the couple who hosted the Wednesday night Bible study in their home.

But those dreams had all come crashing down the day she walked in on her husband looking at pornography on his computer screen. In the dark days that followed, she found out it wasn't just a casual slip but a sexual addiction. And then the final blow—that his addiction hadn't been limited to the computer. Steve stayed in denial, wouldn't get help, and became more abusive than he had been before. Eventually, after a year of turmoil, she had to face the fact that staying with him and forgiving him wasn't going to fix the problem.

Christine pulled into a parking place next to the shabby building where she had an office job. It was the first thing the temp agency had found for her, but she was hoping to get something else soon. At least today was Friday and she could go home at four instead of five and have two whole days with Aubrey and Jacob. She hurried inside the back door, took the elevator up to the eighth floor, and ducked into the tiny office she had already started to hate.

"Hey, Christine!" Her boss did not look happy. "We just got audited. We're going to have to do inventory. Can you stay late tonight?"

Christine hesitated. She could use the extra money from overtime. But then she remembered Jacob's excited smile when she promised him she would make their traditional Friday night hamburgers and french fries after she got off work. She couldn't let him down with everything else going on right now.

"Sorry, Jim, I can't. I have to pick up my kids at five." Christine put her purse under her desk and prayed he wouldn't get angry at her.

He frowned. "Can't you have someone else get them and keep them for a few hours? This is pretty important, and really, the kind of thing I was hoping you'd be available for."

Christine took a deep breath, gripped the side of the plywood desk, and forced her voice to sound professional. "I can't tonight, but if you want me to put in some extra hours next week I'd be glad to."

Jim grunted. "Never mind. I'll find someone else." He started to walk down the hall and then paused and threw a final comment over his shoulder. "I'll call the temp agency and ask them to send someone in who actually cares about doing her job."

Christine sat down numbly in her chair and mechanically logged on to her desktop to check her task list. Her thoughts were frozen for a few minutes. When they gradually began to thaw, they hit up against one another like an ice jam. Had she just lost her job? Would Jim complain to the temp agency? Would they give up on trying to find her another job?

As she scrolled through the office memos in her work e-mail's inbox, she paused at a subject line. "Mother's Day Promotions." Mother's Day. She had totally forgotten it was this Sunday. And what a great Mother's Day present she had gotten, probably losing her job. She bit her lip. *Lord, I need to earn an income. But You gave me children, and that's my first calling. I want to be a good mom and have quality time with my kids. Could You please, somehow, provide a solution where I can do both?*

Christine didn't see Jim again all day; he was obviously avoiding her. Uncertain where she stood, she made sure to finish her task quota and leave her work area tidy. She logged out quietly at four and slipped down to her car. Alone in a safe space at last, she gave herself the luxury of crying for five minutes before she dried her eyes, buckled her seat belt, and ventured out to fight her way through the traffic.

Almost an hour later she pulled up outside Sunshine Day Care and Preschool. Before she got out, she checked her reflection in the visor mirror and smoothed a bit of concealer under her eyes. Aubrey and Jacob were very sensitive to her moods and expressions.

Christine entered the cheerfully decorated center and instantly felt better. Brightly colored children's artwork festooned the freshly painted walls, and neat rows of wooden pegs by the door held little lunch bags.

"Mommy!" Three-year-old Jacob saw her from across the main room, where the children gathered at the end of the day to wait for their parents, and ran toward her. "I made this for you." He held up a big piece of pink construction paper with a red tissue-paper rose crunched on the front. Glittering words, still dripping glue, proclaimed, "Happy Mother's Day!"

Christine knelt down and hugged him. "I love it, sweetie! It's beautiful. Thank you." She buried her nose into his little neck for just a second and breathed in happiness.

"I made you a present too, Mommy. Look at mine!" Aubrey,

just sixteen months older than her brother, came dancing up and offered an artistic creation as well. Her gift was a small bunch of paper flowers on pipe-cleaner stems. Christine took them and hugged her curly-headed daughter. "So pretty! I can't wait to put them in a vase at home."

The school administrator walked over. "Hello, Mrs. Webster. Happy Mother's Day."

Christine stood and smiled. She always enjoyed chatting with Mrs. Martin. The one comforting thing about having to leave her children was the fact that everyone here had been so kind and welcoming. It was worth it to pay over half of her paycheck to get them into this place.

Christine frowned at the thought of money. She didn't even know if she would have a job on Monday.

"Is something wrong?" Mrs. Martin asked.

"Oh, no. I mean, not here. But …" She glanced down at her children. "Can you two go use the bathroom before we go? We have to stop at the grocery store on the way home so I can get the ingredients for our hamburgers." She winked, hoping that reminder would distract them from any lengthy discussion about not needing to go potty.

To her relief, they both dropped their personal items on the floor and ran down the hall.

Christine turned to Mrs. Martin. "I may have a gap between my work assignments from the temp agency," she said, trying to keep it from sounding like a disaster. "If I have a day or two off, can I keep the kids home but still keep their enrollment current?"

"Of course. You'll still have to pay the same monthly fee, though. Same as if they were out for being sick."

Christine knew she wouldn't get a discount, but paying for day care she wasn't using still hurt.

"What kind of work do you do?" Mrs. Martin asked.

"Secretarial, clerical, data entry. Whatever the temp agency assigns me. I have a degree in English, but nothing related to that has opened up so far."

Mrs. Martin glanced toward the main office door, then looked back at Christine. "You know, we're losing our secretary in a couple of weeks. It's a full-time position. We haven't posted the opening yet because we were hoping to find someone we already know rather than have to go through a bunch of interviews with strangers."

Tentative hope sprang up in Christine. "What are the requirements?"

Mrs. Martin smiled. "Honestly, the most important thing is good people skills. The secretary has to interact with all the parents, teachers, and kids on a daily basis. The work itself isn't technical—a lot of answering the phone, e-mailing, and scheduling."

Christine took a deep breath. "How much does it pay?"

Mrs. Martin told her the salary, then added, "And tuition for your kids would be waived."

Christine's thoughts whirled. To work in a positive environment and be near her kids seemed too good to be true. The center was only ten minutes from her apartment, so she wouldn't have to make that awful commute.

"Could I take an application with me?"

"Sure. And I can schedule an interview for ten on Monday, if that works for you."

Christine nodded, and Mrs. Martin hurried to the glass cubicle at the front of the hallway to get an application.

Could this be an answer to the prayer she'd prayed just that morning? If so, it would be one of the fastest responses she'd ever gotten … and the best Mother's Day present ever.

She took the application from Mrs. Martin. "Thank you so much."

Jacob and Aubrey came back, gathered their things, and climbed into the car. As they drove out of the parking lot, Aubrey piped up from the backseat, "I'm so glad it's almost Mother's Day. You're the best mommy in the whole world."

"Yeah," Jacob chimed in. "You make great hamburgers."

Christine's eyes filled with tears for the third time that day. *Thanks, God, for helping me be a good mom.*

Life Application

Life doesn't always go the way we want it to. When mothers go through a crisis, we often feel guilty and wonder how we could ever be a good parent under all that pressure. God cares deeply about us, as well as our children. And He can show us how to parent well, no matter what the circumstances. Isaiah 65:23 says, "They will not work in vain, and their children will not be doomed to misfortune. For they are people blessed by the Lord, and their children, too, will be blessed" (NLT). No matter what trouble we're facing, God will answer our prayers and help us if we call out to Him.

About the Author

Roxanne Anderson spent several years living and doing missionary work in India, Nepal, Hong Kong, and West Africa, and currently lives in Dallas, Texas. Her life is passionately defined by single-parenting three teenagers, her work as a midwife, supporting missions, and writing. She blogs about all these things at roxanneswildworld.blogspot.com.

20

God Blesses Me Too

by Jeanne Marie Leach

"Mrs. Parlow, why didn't you have any children of your own?"

Ardelle smiled at Missy, remembering what it was like to be fifteen years old. She sighed. During all those years of worrying about her infertility, not one person had been direct enough to ask her that simple question.

The teenager munched on one of the brownies she'd baked for her.

"My husband and I didn't have insurance for the first ten years of our marriage, so I never went to the doctor to find out why I couldn't get pregnant. When I could finally afford to get checked out, the doctor said I had a disease called endometriosis … one of the worst cases he'd ever seen."

Missy took her hand. In Ardelle's younger days, people often told her she had pretty hands. Now her skin hugged her bones, paper thin and spotted from old age.

She looked into Missy's eyes and noticed a look of pity. "Now, you stop feeling sorry for me right now, young lady."

Missy scrunched her nose. "But you love children so much. Why didn't you adopt?"

Ardelle remembered the well-meaning yet painful things people used to say to her and Daniel.

You can always adopt.

What are you waiting for?

If you don't try so hard, you'll get pregnant.

This is what worked for my sister-in-law, so I know it will work for you.

I read an article the other day about this new device your husband can wear and they guarantee you'll get pregnant.

If you just had more faith …

She'd forgiven those people long ago. "We tried adoption three times, but on each occasion something came up that prevented it."

"Why didn't you keep trying?"

"We couldn't afford to. The filing fees are very expensive."

Missy looked like she was trying to understand. "My Sunday school teacher told me the Bible says a man is blessed when his quiver is full. That means having lots of children. She said she felt bad for anyone who wasn't blessed."

"Goodness, child!" Ardelle marveled at the inaccuracies people spread throughout the community and the church. "God blesses me too. In fact, He has blessed me in ways that some people with children will never know."

"Really?" Missy's eyes grew wide.

"Have another brownie and I'll tell you about it." Ardelle lifted the small plate and held it up to her young friend.

The girl smiled broadly. "Thanks." She grabbed her second treat and placed it on her saucer. "Could I get more milk too?"

"Of course, dear."

While Ardelle waited for Missy to return from the kitchen, she picked up scattered brownie crumbs from the tiny coffee table. She never thought she'd enjoy living in this efficiency apartment, but it hadn't taken her long to adjust. Everything was much handier here than in the big house on Chestnut Lane she'd shared with Daniel for over fifty-five years. Although he'd been living in heaven for nearly ten years now, Ardelle still missed him.

Missy returned and set her glass of milk on a coaster, then balanced her saucer on her lap. "Okay, I'm ready to hear the story."

Ardelle supposed one never outgrew the love of hearing a good story. "This happened around forty-five years ago. Daniel and I were in our early thirties. We'd been married for seven years and were living in an apartment in Oklahoma City." Ardelle recalled the incident as if it had happened yesterday.

"Daniel played in a garage band, and they had a gig in Texas one weekend. I taught kindergarten Sunday school back then, so I went to church alone that time. It was the last day before kindergarten graduation. I dismissed the children early so their new teacher could take them down the hall and show them where their classroom would be the following Sunday.

"The children lined up in excitement and marched single

file out the door behind their new teacher. The last boy in line turned just as he was about to exit. I'll never forget the look on his face. 'Will I ever see you again?' he asked.

"'Of course,' I told him. 'We'll see each other in church all the time.' Satisfied with my answer, he turned and walked out of the classroom. But my heart broke at the loss of those children, and at not having one of my own."

Ardelle sipped her iced tea. Missy gave her that pity look again, but she chose to ignore it. "I went home that day and stomped all around our apartment, shaking my fist at God and yelling at Him. 'Why can't I have children of my own?' I demanded. 'Why do You always give me kids I fall in love with and then have to give back to their parents?' Then something miraculous happened."

Missy's brownie lay untouched on her plate. She leaned toward Ardelle.

"As sure as I'm talking to you now, God spoke to me. Not audibly, like He did with Saint Paul in the Bible, but inside." Ardelle pointed a finger toward her heart. "He told me that I would have been a wonderful mother. But He gave me a special gift of working with other people's children, and He wanted to use that."

"Couldn't God have given you both?" Missy asked.

"Yes, He could have." Ardelle nodded. "But if I became a mother, I'd concentrate all my efforts on my own family. There would be nothing wrong with that. But God wanted to give me hundreds of children so I could make a difference in all their lives."

Missy's face lit up. "Like me!"

"That's right, dear. You're one of my God-sent children. Actually, you're part of phase two of His plan for me."

"Phase two?"

"When Daniel and I were in our fifties, we built an addition to our house so more children could come visit us. We called it the bunkhouse because it had two sets of bunk beds. I had so much fun decorating it."

"And did more people come?" Missy's anticipation tickled Ardelle.

"They sure did. As a matter of fact, those bunk beds got a lot of use over the next fifteen years. And one day, as I made up the beds, God talked to me again."

"He did?" Missy shoved a bite of brownie into her mouth without taking her eyes off Ardelle. "What did He say?"

"He told me He was going to give me and Daniel grandchildren to bless us in our old age."

"But how could that happen if you were never a mother?"

Ardelle patted Missy's hand. "Because we had more room, families with children began staying with us. A few of those children still visit me from time to time."

Missy frowned. "I wish I could have stayed in your bunk beds."

Ardelle patted the floral cushion beneath her. "This sofa is a sleeper."

Missy's eyes sparkled. "Is that an invitation?"

"You're welcome to stay with me anytime."

The girl stood and kissed Ardelle's cheek. "I could get my things and stay with you tonight if that's okay."

"If your parents agree, it's all right with me."

"Awesome!" She gave Ardelle a big hug. "Would you mind if I brought my friend Kathy to stay tonight too? Her parents are divorced and she doesn't know Christ. I think she'd learn a lot from you."

Ardelle smiled. "Of course, dear. If she gets permission from her parents, of course."

"Got it."

Missy scurried out of the apartment with a huge grin.

Ardelle pulled her bifocals off her nose and wiped her eyes with the handkerchief she kept tucked in her sleeve. *Thank You, Lord. You are so faithful to me. You've kept all Your promises … even after fifty years.*

"And Lord, it looks like You're sending me one more child to love." Ardelle padded to the kitchen to bake another batch of brownies.

Life Application

God chooses to bless us in different ways. And God is big; there is no limit to what He can do. He can speak a baby into existence. He can use modern medicine to help a couple have a child. He can provide the means for adoption. His plan for some couples may not include children.

Don't think someone isn't blessed just because he or she

doesn't have what you have. God may be blessing that person in bigger ways than you can imagine.

If you know a woman who doesn't have natural or adopted children, take the time to get to know her. You may discover that she has a mother's heart after all.

About the Author

Jeanne Marie Leach is a multipublished Christian fiction author, a freelance editor, and a teacher of online fiction editing courses at The Christian PEN: Proofreaders and Editors Network. She is also a member of the Christian Editor Connection and American Christian Fiction Writers. She lives with her husband of forty-one years and their Alaskan malamute, Kona, in beautiful Colorado.

21

But I Still Love You

by Julie DeEtte Williams

I'm too old to be a mother again. I mean, diapers and tantrums and "Can I drive the car?" were hard enough in my twenties and thirties. But now?

As I pull into the garage, the decibels coming from the television rattle my car windows. I drag myself from the vehicle. After an eight-hour shift on my feet, another confrontation is the last thing I need.

"Turn the volume down, Mom," I holler above the raucous antics of whatever reality TV show she's found.

No response. She must have forgotten to put in her hearing aids … again.

I tap on her shoulder and mouth my request.

She fumbles with the remote and punches buttons. One channel up, two down, up again, and finally she hits the blessed mute button. She pats the sofa cushion next to her. "Sit down, Geraldine. You have to see this."

Another stab in my chest. Today Mom thinks I'm her aunt, Scary Geri.

I do the one thing I hated as a kid. I step between my mother and the TV to get her full attention. "Mom, I'm Deb—" A new pang steals all my breath.

The left side of her chin is caked in dry blood. My knees aren't sure they can hold my weight.

I plop down on the hassock and almost knock it over. "How on earth did you do that?"

She touches it with a wadded-up, soiled napkin clutched in her fist. "The doctor on TV said I would burn more calories skipping than running."

"You skipped down the block?"

"Oh, no. What would the neighbors think? I went on the treadmill." She dabs her chin again. "It doesn't like skipping."

"I should think not. How about you stick to walking on it instead?"

She nods, but I don't quite believe her.

"Let's get you cleaned up and make sure that doesn't become infected." I lead her by the hand to the bathroom and help her sit on the toilet lid.

I soak a cotton ball in peroxide and propagate the lie Mom often told me. The one I spread to my kids. "This won't hurt a bit." I dab it to her chin.

She whimpers and blinks. Little tears run the maze of her age lines.

My cheeks are damp too.

With Mom finally settled in her room, I schlep into the

kitchen. Someone has to make dinner, although I doubt I could stomach a bite. The light on the answering machine blinks, so I hit the play button.

"Deborah. Your mother's been butchering my prize roses again. She's over here every bleeping Wedn—"

I hit the delete button and swallow another bad word. What's one rose a week if it makes an old lady happy?

The counter is littered with Little Debbie wrappers. Really? She can eat these every day and not remember my name is Debbie? I open the refrigerator door and slam it shut. "Mom, why didn't you eat the salad I made for your lunch?"

"It was green." Her voice floats back from my office.

Terrific. What's she into now? I can't bring myself to look, so I pop two cups of soup into the microwave and throw together a grilled cheese sandwich for us to split.

When dinner's finished, I broach the subject we both dread. "It's time for your bath."

"I don't want to."

"It's not an option." I bite my tongue before a my house, my rules can slip out.

She pouts. No kidding. And drags her feet like a three-year-old all the way to the shower.

An hour and a half later, scrubbed, dried, jammied, and tucked in bed, Mom gives me the sad-eyes and quivering-lip treatment. "I'm not tired."

"Yes, but I am, and I have to get up and go to work in the morning."

"Read me a story." She holds out the book she used to read to me.

Now we've come full circle—from *Goodnight Moon* to *Caddie Woodlawn* to *Pride and Prejudice* and *Bleak House*, and back to Margaret Wise Brown.

I open the worn cardboard cover. "In the great green room …"[1] My voice catches in my throat every time I read this line, and Mom's soft tones recite it along with me.

Somehow I make it to the end of the book and am rewarded by a chorus of my mother's soft snores.

I brush a wispy white curl from her forehead and give it a kiss, the way I did with my children—something I learned from her, no doubt. She's an angel when she's sleeping.

My cell phone chirps and I swipe it to silent as I creep out of the room to answer the call. My daughter's face appears on the screen. "Hi, Karissa. What's up?"

"Hey, Mom. Just calling to check on Grandma. Did she know who you were today?"

Bitter words spring to my tongue, but I swallow them down. Someday the circle will connect and my daughter will play the role of mother to me. "Pray for her, Kari. It must be hard to forget so much."

"Of course I will." My daughter hesitates. "Have you thought any more about putting her in a rest home?"

"Only when the TV's on at full blast. So yeah, every hour

---

1   Margaret Wise Brown, *Goodnight Moon* (first published by Harper & Brothers, 1947).

of every day." My laughter turns into a shudder. I could never put my mom through that. I've seen too much of those places. Even one of the really good homes would be hard on her. "You know I think that assisted-living facilities are a good option for some people. But your grandmother is too … active. She'd shrivel up if she couldn't spend half her day walking in the sunshine." And the other half annoying me.

My phone buzzes. "I gotta go. There's another call coming in. Love you!" I swipe to the new call.

Harsh words bordering on profanity fill my ear. I should learn not to pick up the phone without checking caller ID.

"Every Wednesday …"

I glance in at Mom's bureau. A single rose crowns the faded flowers from weeks gone by.

"I won't stand for it. Control your mother or I will!"

Tears prick my eyes while I wait for the tirade to sputter out, gathering the courage to say what I should have said the first time Mom nabbed one of the neighbor's roses. "I am very sorry. But I don't know how to stop her. I don't actually want to stop her. You see, my dad died on a Wednesday."

I take the stark silence on the other end of the line as permission to hang up and crawl into bed.

Did Mom have days like this one when she was raising us and half the neighborhood?

Definitely.

Grace for tomorrow—that will be my prayer tonight.

"Good morning, Mom," I say in a cheery voice. "Do you know who I am today?"

She looks me up and down, head tilted to the right, then to the left. She stares at me like a lost little girl, and I feel the pain deep in my chest.

I sit on the edge of the bed and help her rise. "I'm Debbie. Your middle daughter."

"No, you're not. I found you last night." She pulls her large-print King James Bible into her lap and taps the page she bookmarked. "Here. It's you."

Pink crayon marks Psalm 30:5. "Joy cometh in the morning."

Her cheeks raise her lips into a sly smile. Well, at least her sense of humor is still intact.

"Okay, Mom, I'll be Joy today." The dull ache melts into a laugh. I wrap my arms around her.

She wiggles out of my embrace and scratches the side of her head. "*Somefing* bit me."

It's gum. Chewed. How did she manage it, with her teeth grinning up at me from the glass on the nightstand?

"Where on earth did you get that?"

She points to her purse. "Paulie gave it to me."

Great-Grandpa Paul? Mom's really reaching back in time today. There's no use holding an interrogation. Clearly the minimart was on yesterday's route.

There ought to be a law. *"Gum?"* The clerk would look his patron square in her wrinkled face. *I'll have to card you for that. You were born before 1930. Sorry, ma'am, I can't sell you matches, sharp objects, or puppies, either.*

For now, I'll confiscate whatever's left when she's not looking and maybe—just maybe—she'll forget that too.

When I touch the offending wad, she screams like I'm scalping her.

"Get dressed, Mom, and then we'll see about getting that fixed." I trot out of her room before I can give in to the temptation to dig the scissors out of her sewing basket and exact my revenge for a dozen bad haircuts at her hand.

I can't live like this. It's time for a new tactic. I snatch up the phone, dial, and work up a composed tone.

"Peace and Light Assisted Living. How may I direct your call?"

"Teddy, it's Debbie. I …"

Mom pads into the kitchen with a fresh box of Little Debbies. She tears open the carton and hands me the first one.

"Debbie, are you there?"

"Yeah, sorry, Teddy. I need to take a personal day. Can you find someone to cover my shift today?" Tomorrow I'll broach the subject of dropping back to part time.

"Sure. Are you okay?"

"I'm fine." The stress is already rolling off my shoulders. "I need to take my mother in for a haircut. Then I think I'll spend the rest of the day with her at the zoo."

Mom takes my cheeks in her arthritic hands and pulls my face to hers. "I'm not sure who you are."

"I know." I drop the receiver onto the base without hearing Teddy's reply.

Mom kisses my cheek. "But I still love you."

Life Application

My grandmother gave me a piece of amazing advice when my children were particularly rambunctious. "Spend an afternoon in a children's hospital and you'll appreciate what you have."

Whether you're raising children, parenting your parents, or cultivating a trying relationship, one thing is true—nothing stays the same forever. Children grow up, parents age and meet the Lord, some relationships bloom and others die. Through it all, God doesn't change—He's there for you. Trust Him through the hard times and enjoy every minute He gives you with friends and family.

"My God will meet all your needs according to the riches of his glory in Christ Jesus" (Philippians 4:19).

How can you celebrate the relationships God has given you?

In what ways might you need to look at your circumstances from a new perspective?

Are there needs in your life that only God can supply?

About the Author

Julie Williams works as a freelance editor and typographer for Inspire Press. She writes historical fiction, dabbles in allegory, and is trying her hand at fairy tale. On her days off, she enjoys wandering the gardens at the Huntington Library with her husband. Most Fridays you can find her at Disneyland. On the Web, you can find her at http://juliewilliams.us.

by Kathy Ide

As you've seen from these stories, mothers come in many varieties. Biological moms. Adoptive moms. Stepmothers. Grandmothers. Godmothers. Even "second moms"—women who invest in our lives the way a "real" mother would, at least for a season. Even a dad can act as a mom for a child when life circumstances put him in that position.

I had a great mother and a happy childhood, free of dysfunction and abuse—little realizing at the time how unusual that was. Today, most people I know struggle to overcome issues related to neglect, abuse, even abandonment from their family of origin. But there was one thing I knew, without a shadow of doubt, as I was going up: my parents loved me.

A funny thing happened when I was an adolescent, though. My mom changed, practically overnight, into a rule nazi. She implemented a curfew—even for prom night. Inconceivable! She refused to let me drive alone into Minneapolis for an event that lasted till almost midnight. What was wrong with her? And if my boyfriend came over, she insisted the bedroom door stay open. Did she think I couldn't be trusted?

Using my own highly developed judgmental skills, I defied some of her rules … and got grounded for it. When she caught me.

A few times, I became so upset with my mom that I shouted, "I hate you!" and stormed down the hall to my room, slamming the door so hard the walls trembled.

Another funny thing happened when I had my first child. Again my mother made a major transformation. This time, she suddenly became amazingly wise, compassionate, and patient. Whenever I had a question or concern about what to do with my son, all I had to do was pick up the phone and call her. She always gave me good advice, calmed me down, and helped me work through the problem. And she repeatedly reminded me that "this too shall pass." Especially when my kids seemed to hate me for the decisions I made that I believed were best for them.

I'm in my "empty nest" season now. (Although, since I live in Southern California, my nest isn't actually empty very much of the time. My husband and I regularly have relatives come to visit and take in the local tourist attractions. Both sides of the family have told us repeatedly that we are not allowed to move! Not that we would—we love being the "Ide Bed-and-Breakfast" for them.) I am extremely blessed to have healthy relationships with both of my adult sons.

And my mom? Well, she seems to have made yet another transition. She's now my friend.

Whether you have positive or negative memories of your mother (biological, adoptive, step–, or substitute mom), a healthy or unhealthy relationship with her, or even if your mom isn't part of your life anymore … and whether or not you're a mother yourself … I hope the stories in this book have blessed you.

If you have been impacted by any of the stories in this book, may I encourage you to share that experience with others? Visit our website, FictionDevo.com, and find the forum on "21 Days of Joy." Read what others have said about the stories in this book, and post something yourself about what a particular story meant to you.

If you prefer a more casual setting, visit facebook.com/FictionDevo to read and write posts about all of the books in the Fiction Lover's Devotional series.

More Books in this Series

Look for more books in this series
from BroadStreet Publishing

21 Days of Grace:
Stories that Celebrate God's Unconditional Love

21 Days of Christmas:
Stories that Celebrate God's Greatest Gift

21 Days of Love:
Stories that Celebrate Treasured Relationships

Alphabetical List of Contributing Authors